REDISCOVERING EMOTION

DAVID PUGMIRE

EDINBURGH UNIVERSITY PRESS

For PV

© David Pugmire, 1998

Edinburgh University Press
22 George Square, Edinburgh

Phototypeset in Goudy by Intype London Ltd
Printed and bound in Great Britain
by MPG Books Ltd, Bodmin

A CIP record for this book is available from the British Library

ISBN 0 7486 1126 6 (paperback)

The right of David Pugmire
to be identified as author of this work
has been asserted in accordance with
the Copyright, Designs and Patents Act 1988.

Contents

Acknowledgements

The reflections, and even the reading, out of which this book has grown owe much to the advice, comment and the criticisms of others. Over time I have tried to assimilate responses to various parts of it read or heard by Aaron Ridley, Robert Roberts, Martin Hollis, David Black and David Owen. Special thanks are due to Alex Neill, who not only read the typescript in both an earlier and a later version but also discussed it with me in detail over several roasting but memorable days in San Antonio. Finally, the production of the text itself would scarcely have happened without numerous patient interventions by Wendy Williams.

I wish to thank the *Journal of Philosophy and Phenomenological Research* for permission to quote from my article 'Real Emotion' (vol. 54, 1994), parts of which appear in Chapter 8 of this book. I would also like to thank the estate of George Orwell, Martin Secker & Warburg Ltd, Harcourt Brace & Company and A. M. Heath & Co. Ltd for permission to use passages from *Coming up for Air*, which are Copyright (©) Mark Hamilton as the Literary Executor of the Estate of the Late Sonia Brownell Orwell.

Introduction

– EMOTION –

The problems raised by emotion are both theoretical and real. It is a truth so basic as to go unremarked that emotion quickens the occupations of life, transfiguring what would otherwise be a web of bare tasks. Into these it insinuates affection, pride, reverence, alarm, ire, verve, languor. Jonathan Swift's Houyhnhnms do not grieve for their dead because they do not rejoice in their living. Our emotional susceptibilities do not just reflect our concerns. They also create ways in which things and events acquire interest for us. Indeed, emotions may themselves become sources of beguilement, a fact which exposes them to corruption. On the other hand, particular emotions (indeed, emotion itself) often appear as the enemies of good sense, as dangerous or demeaning visitations. In contrast to sound judgement and settled intentions they are apt to seem either volatile ('There I go again') or effervescent ('Sorry, I'm off the boil'); unaccountable and renegade ('Then why am I so depressed/calm/ frightened?') and therefore unpredictable; and, of course, intractable – hard to control once they get a grip. Worse still, when they are roused it is notoriously hard not to be controlled by them. They have the power to prevail over the 'steadier' faculties. They can even move from successfully opposing better judgement to commandeering it – that is, they can deflect it into their service in the shape of rationalisation, enslaving reason itself by engendering self-deceit.

These truisms about the emotions reflect an equation of emotion with active states of emotional feeling and encourage a primordial theoretical conception of it as a kind of energy or force. Hence the common metaphors of tempest and tide. Such thoughts make up the idea of emotion as *passion*. The history of the word 'emotion' in English converges on this idea. The *Oxford English Dictionary* records the change from 'emotion' as a 'moving out' to a (physical) stirring or agitation to (figuratively) 'Any agitation or disturbance of mind, feeling, passion; any vehement or excited mental state' and, as a term of psychology, 'A mental "feeling" or "affection" . . . as distinguished from cognitive or volitional states of consciousness. *abstr.* "feeling" as distinct from the other classes of mental phenomena.'

The difficulties experienced with emotions can raise questions about the nature of emotion. Whence its power to sway? How, and how far, is it opposed to reason? Is it educable? – Surprisingly, the extent to which the traditional equation of emotion with passion survives reflection on these questions remains unclear.

– THE PHILOSOPHY OF EMOTION –

Emotions exhibit a tempting spectrum of properties. The theorist is spoilt for choice. Yet these properties are not all equally accommodating conceptually, nor therefore philosophically inviting to the same degree. Leading examples, in decreasing order of tractability, are:

Cognitions. These range from outright belief or judgement, for example, that I am imperilled, or that I am free at last or that I am undone, to the mere thought of something as having a feature without actually judging or believing that it has (the mere or very thought of something). Such non-assertional thought includes imagining (for example, purely notional dangers), the sway of imagery and even perception that is not propositional ('Just something in that *look!*').

Valuations. These may be judgements, as in admiration or disdain ('What a lucid speech!'/'How craven!'). Or they may be non-judgemental, as with

Desires, for example, lust; or pinings and yearnings to which value-judgements might lead.

Affect or *feeling*. The sharp or dull edge of an emotion, its crescendos and diminuendos – in other words, its passion, where present, and the qualities of that, as evinced variously in, for example, euphoria, dejection, anguish or affection.[1]

The respective salience of these factors varies across the varieties of emotion and in individual occurrences of them. Thus, emotions are not necessarily passionate or sharply felt (tranquillity), nor do they have to incorporate desires, even when, as in sadness, they presuppose some desires and may lead to others. But the aim of theoretical understanding would be nicely served if some of them could be assimilated to others; or best of all, if a subset of the more perspicuous and philosophically trusty of these factors turned out to be pivotal to what an emotion is, at least in paradigmatic cases. The rest could be left as occasional and incidental accompaniments of emotion, undeserving of special attention. In any such contest, cognitions are surprisingly fitted to win.

And so they have. Philosophers, especially those in the analytic tradition, have concentrated on the ways in which emotions embody thoughts, including appraisals, and trade on them for their identity. Thus, certain thoughts seem fundamental to given emotions: for example, 'How outrageous' for anger, or, for fear, 'It doesn't bear thinking about but here it comes!' And if emotion is more than mere contemplation, the valuational loading of the portraying thoughts accounts for that: the emotively salient thoughts may be valuational in character ('Your remarks were cruel, outrageously so!').[2] In philosophy, the idea that emotions may be treated as types of thought, judgemental *or* non-judgmental, has become almost an orthodoxy. For many purposes, indeed, this is a convenient, even an illuminating way of regarding them, and as such is an interesting revision of the pre-philosophical view of emotion.

Passion, the urgency in emotion, its affective tone that strikes the philosophically uninitiated as what is emotional about emotions, has typically been left at the periphery of philosophical discussion (when not outside it altogether). But there are dissenters. A number of writers have observed that certain less straightforward cases of emotion seem both embued with passion and at variance with what the person's relevant judgements, at any rate, would call for.[3] Yet this might create the risk that feeling, as something psychically potent but cognitively opaque might have a central role in a sufficient range of emotional phenomena to have to be taken seriously in the philosophy of mind – a prospect at which many would flinch. Such a notion could seem an uninviting atavism considering the strides modern philosophy has taken against Cartesianism.

Hence the importance of the work of dissenters from judgementalism who are alert to these challenges presented by emotional affect. For they have tried to show how even the phenomenon of emotive feeling can be rendered in terms of non-judgmental thoughts, and the ways these bear on the mind. Perhaps episodes of feeling are themselves thoughts in which something is construed in charged ways (for example, as charmingly innocent or as sinister); or perhaps they are thoughts to which pain or pleasure attach.[4] These treatments offer to extend the writ of a liberal cognitivism from one end of the spectrum of emotion-attributes to the other, a redeeming prospect for many.

– THE PROJECT –

The pervading aim of the present work is the restoration of emotional affect, or feeling, as a free-standing, working concept in understanding emotion. The structure of this study has roughly the order which thinking about the emotions has followed in philosophy over the last thirty years. It examines the several strands of cognition (mentioned above) that contribute to emotion. My claim is that the attempt to understand emotions in terms of one or another type of thought, however instructive, finally fails. It either obscures the dimension of affect or misrepresents it, notwithstanding the ingenious efforts of some writers to avoid this.

I start (in the first two chapters) by introducing emotive cognitivism in what might be called its classical form in which emotions are held to comprise judgements and beliefs. In Chapters 2 and 3, the resources of this approach are then tested against the problems posed by irrational emotion and the quantitative feature of (variable) intensity, which emotions have. These resources are in fact deeper than critics have often realised. Refinements in the types of cognition that might be involved are also tested against these problems, especially *value*-judgements and the non-judgemental and aspectual thoughts. Revealing though these can be of the emotively stirred mind, there are features of emotions that elude them (and even their close relation, desire). I contend that the notion of emotive feeling, does, however, make sense of these potentials (Chapter 4).

The question then becomes how much of a grip on *that* (the flash of anger, the blackness of despair) a cognitive analysis can hope to secure. What kind of thoughts could *engage* us as emotions do and how? – A theory of emotive thoughts that could fill the role of feeling or affect has been something of a Grail in recent philosophy of emotion. In Chapter 5, I urge that it is not to be found, however absorbing the quest.

Many hopes have been pinned on thoughts of a specifically *valuational* sort. Emotions are ways we have of *minding* things, and the key to this may be sought in our appraisals. The role of valuational thoughts in the genesis and even composition of a person's emotions has been the focus of much recent literature. This can be seen either as superseding more traditional cognitivism or as a refinement of it. (Appraisals seem cognitive in as much as they involve ascribing importance or value to events and so tend to be assertional or quasi-assertional.) In any case, as a promising bridge between perceived fact and its emotive impact, they invite special attention. In the above chapters, the suggestion is developed that emotions themselves comprise a sui generis type of valuation. This means that where one can speak of 'evaluative patterns constituting the nature of the given emotion',[5] the nature of the evaluation must be understood in terms of the nature of emotion, not the other way around. But that will make it less easy to regard appraisal as a 'component' of emotion that is distinct from feeling.

If the argument of these chapters is correct, those familiar touchstones of interpretation in the philosophy of mind, belief and desire, will not avail for the emotions. In this way, the philosophy of emotion bears on the question of the simplicity of the mind. Do what we pre-reflectively identify as emotions dissolve into an array of antecedent psychological phenomena or do they require an extension of the range of phenomena that must be recognised? A careful examination of emotions, I suggest, favours greater complexity.

Thus, a substantive account of emotive feeling is needed which does not centre primarily on cognitions of any sort. But a psychologically realistic treatment of feeling has its philosophical pitfalls, both real and apparent, which have stood in its way, and these must be negotiated. A beginning is made with these tasks in Chapters 6 and 7: what constitutes a feeling as much as anything is its subjective character as experienced (as distinct from the thoughts that may make for it). Yet, taking subjectivity seriously here, I argue, does not entail a reversion to epistemological privacy and Dualism. The device of metaphor allows the fluid nuances of feeling to be captured in the public language.

The difference between thought and feeling is of moment as well as of interest. In Chapter 8 it is applied to show how *false* emotion is possible and to bring out a disciplining role that belief can have. If *too* great a part is given to emotional feeling in *practice*, some emotions can lose their integrity. Some emotions are susceptible to failure of authenticity. Thus, the distracting vivacity of emotive feeling can prompt an identification of one's emotions with one's feelings. This can be an illusion and a motivated lapse. Here, at least, the spell of feeling ungirded by thought is an actual fault in living, but one which it takes philosophical diagnosis to understand. Cognition has a *normative* role to play in the life of the emotions that only emerges properly when cognitive *theories* of emotion loosen their grip.

These are the matters to which we must now turn.

– NOTES –

1. Readiness to act might serve better than desire here, as being that which a desire rouses in the person. Bodily arousal might be inserted alongside psychic affect or even in place of it as being what feelings of emotion amount to.
2. Bedford (1956) and Solomon (1977) established well-known versions of this approach. More recently, judgements of value have become the favoured candidates for the thoughts that distinguish emotional states. See, for instance, Nussbaum (1993), Oakley (1992) and Ben-Ze'ev (1997).
3. As Stocker (1983) and Leighton (1985) point out.
4. As urged, respectively, by Roberts (1988), Budd (1985) and Greenspan (1988).
5. Ben-Ze'ev (1997), p. 137.

CHAPTER 1

Emotion and Thought

> Now boys, I know that at a time like this there's gonna be some
> personal emotions that you'll be thinkin'.
>
> B52 pilot in *Dr Strangelove*

– THE HANDMAIDEN OF THOUGHT –

Contrary to common wisdom, emotion and thought do not displace one
another. Emotion is bound up with thought in a host of ways. Emotions
may be kindled by a memory or realisation. On the other hand, an
emotion may govern one's train of reflection and ordain one's beliefs, as
prejudice and wishful thinking testify. Such relations of influence are
obvious enough. But the ties between emotion and cognition can be
deeper still. To one who hopes or who suffers disappointment, things have
a certain shape. Recognitions, convictions, imaginings, memories and
valuings are woven into emotions, internal to them, and somehow thereby
enlivened. Maybe emotions just are thoughts that in some sense burn
bright. What could this mean?

There are two questions here: What form or forms does thought take
when it enters emotions? And how, or how far, can the awakening of
sentiment – the *emotive* quality – in emotion be confected out of its
cognitive commitments?

– EMOTION'S FULCRUM? –

Belief, or judgement, seems an obvious hinge on which emotions turn,
and it is the first form of thought to be exploited by cognitive theorists
of emotion. It is safe to say that the full nature of its role in emotion is
still not fully clear (see final chapter). However, that the limits of my
beliefs can be limits to my emotions is immediately striking. A condition
of *hope* is a belief in the possibility of what is hoped for and in its worth.
Where the beliefs in desirability and personal connection appropriate to

pride make no sense, *pride* is impossible. I could not be proud of a distant star, and the impossibility here is more than psychological.

A salient difference between most of the states we regard as emotions and physical sensations is that the latter do not *represent* their causes (medical diagnosis would be the easier if they did). Tingles, itches, nausea are brute presences, in themselves opaque to the rest of the world, including what gives rise to them. They carry in themselves no message as to what is impinging on the person to produce them. By contrast, fear, hope, pride, regret, joy and depression each bespeak a characteristic shape to things outside themselves.

In consequence, there would appear to be something grossly wanting in the idea that emotion is bare passion. This has been the instructive verdict of most philosophers and many psychologists who have interested themselves in the nature of emotion in recent times. In fact, one of the salient achievements of the philosophy of mind in the last decades has been the reappraisal of emotion. Latter-day discussions of emotion tend to unite in rejecting the traditional separation of reason from passion and the equation of emotion with passion. David Hume had expressed that traditional conception of emotion as well as anyone:

> A passion is an original existence, or, if you will, modification of existence, and contains not any representative quality, which renders it a copy of any other existence or modification. When I am angry, I am actually possest with the passion, and in that emotion have no more a reference to any other object, than when I am thirsty, or sick, or more than five foot high, 'Tis impossible, therefore, that this passion can be oppos'd by, or be contradictory to truth or reason; since this contradiction consists in the disagreement of ideas, considered as copies, with those objects, which they represent . . . nothing can be contrary to truth or reason, except what has a reference to it, and . . . the judgements of our understanding only have this reference . . .[1]

What has seemed fatal to the idea that, again as Hume put it, emotions are 'original facts and realities, compleat in themselves, and implying no reference' is the idea that thoughts are actually *integral* to emotions.[2] Emotion can be seen to belong to our rational capacities, as being one way our rationality expresses itself.

In the more straightforward cases, this is a matter of beliefs and judgements which the emotions incorporate. The type of emotion that an emotion is seems fixed by the relevant thoughts its host has, which are often beliefs he accepts or judgements he reaches.[3] So perhaps to each kind of emotion, there is a 'logic', a distinctive pattern of implications, expressible in propositional form, as noted above in the case of pride; and that is what distinguishes it from other kinds of emotion. 'It is a psychological truism that men do not, with some exceptions, hope their opponents will win; it is a truth of logic that they cannot hope that their opponents will win without approving of this in some respect.'[4] For a more complex case, consider Jon Elster's anatomy of indignation at unfair treatment:

> Sufficient conditions for the occurrence of this powerful emotion are the following. First, the situation is perceived as morally wrong; second, it has been brought about intentionally, not as the by-product of natural causality or the invisible hand of social causality; third, it can be rectified by social intervention. Thus the feeling of injustice rests on the combination of 'It ought to be otherwise,' 'It is someone's fault that it is not otherwise' and 'It could be made otherwise'. When one of the conditions is lacking, envy or resentment may arise instead.[5]

Actually, there are several kinds of belief out of which an emotion may be woven. There may be a belief about what the emotion is directed at (whom I resent), about its reason (what I resent), about its cause (why I should be resentful of that) and about the identity of my emotion (that I *resent*). Any of these beliefs may be wrong. Not all of them need be present (free-floating emotions such as anxiety may involve no more than an identifying belief). The point is, there are constraints on what kind of beliefs can betoken a given kind of emotion, particularly the beliefs that articulate the reasons for the emotion.[6] Thus, its complement of beliefs provides both variety and unity to the forms that a given emotion takes.

To the extent that our emotions are a function of our beliefs, they are as perspicuous as our beliefs. The world conveys itself through them, and the emotions will necessarily alter in keeping with relevant changes in our understanding of the world. If they are also a function of our *value-judgements* on the world as we believe it to be, then they will further respond (and be responsible) to the development of our moral and aesthetic sensitivity. Thus, far from being alien and impervious to Reason, and to be shunned in preference to it, emotions are tractable to insight and susceptible to revision and refinement in its wake because they are continuous with cognitive assent and dissent.

– CONSOLIDATING JUDGEMENTALISM –

A representational or cognitive conception of emotion plainly requires a strong tie of some order between what we think and the emotions that we have. Where the thoughts are judgements or beliefs, just what could this tie be?

If a person's beliefs decide the identity of his emotions, having the right beliefs for a given emotion is 'part of the very concept' of having that emotion.[7] So that for someone with that emotion to have these beliefs is 'a truth of logic'.[8] Now, this logical tie could take at least two forms. For a person to have an emotion might entail that he holds certain beliefs. Or more strongly, an emotion might be identical with the beliefs (or with holding them) and entail them for that reason. Some philosophers have been prepared to endorse this stronger thesis explicitly:

> What is an emotion? An emotion is a judgement . . . Something we do . . . A change in my beliefs . . . entails (not causes) a change in my emotion . . . My anger is that set of judgements. Similarly, my embarrassment is my judgement to the effect that I am in an exceedingly awkward situation . . . The judgements and objects that constitute our emotions are those which are especially important to us, meaningful to us, concerning matters in which we have invested our Selves.[9]

Notice that even the humbler claim, that having an emotion merely entails that the person having it make certain judgements, is bolder than it looks if it doesn't allow for anything else the emotion is or that having it essentially involves. It would seem then just to become the strong thesis that the emotion *is* its constituent judgements.

– WHAT ABOUT FEELING? –

That emotional *feelings* – the ways we are *stirred* by emotion, emotion's *edge* – have not figured in our portrait of emotion so far is no oversight. Perhaps somehow judgement itself can do the work of passion, or if not, then perhaps thought in some other guise still holds the key! Thus, when people avow emotions, so often the actual focus of what they say is not on their inward state of mind, on the nuances of feeling passing through them, but on what evokes the emotion and what *it* is like ('Your failure to show up was contemptible, a bitter disappointment to us all'). 'How I adore that dress' needn't be meant autobiographically. Even explicit references to how one is feeling can serve obliquely to describe the source of the emotion: 'I've never felt so furious' is a way of indicating just how outrageous the offence was. Emotion words belong to the vocabulary of critical evaluation.

There is enough truth to this to encourage those who are impressed by it to disregard emotional feeling altogether. Writing in 1980, the psychologist R. B. Zajonc noted that 'Contemporary cognitive psychology simply ignores affect. The words *affect, attitude, emotion, feeling* and *sentiment* do not appear in the indexes of any of the major works on cognition.' And he notes that in a work on language and perception, Miller and Johnson-Laird on the one hand acknowledge that '*Feel* is an indispensable predicate for any complete psychology and that it probably lies much closer than *Perceive, Remember, Intend* to the basic sources of energy that keep the whole system running' and yet confess that 'Nevertheless, we will have little to say about *Feel* in the following pages.'[10]

Of course the fact that avowals of emotion need not convey inward-looking psychic information doesn't mean that they cannot. But would information about states of feeling shed much light on a person's *emotions* in any case? Perhaps not. Feelings may be alleged to lack several important features that emotions have. (In reviewing these, I will add caveats that signal the need for deeper consideration of the issue.)

Here are feeling's failings:

1. Like the shuddering symptomatic of an illness, a feeling (tension, excitement, listlessness) just happens and cannot be evaluated for appropriateness, reasonableness or justification. If emotions were feelings, that would 'not allow the notions of reasonableness and justifiability to gain any foothold in the concept of an emotion'.[11] Emotions (disappointment, nostalgia, pride) can be silly, unfair, outrageous, wanting, called for and so on, but sheer feelings (melancholy, wistfulness, ecstasy) can't.

   Preliminary caveat: It is not obvious that this is true. Couldn't excitement be found inappropriate (uncalled for, bizarre) in the absence of anything exciting? Couldn't we find a thrill (for example, sparked by cruelty) indecent or perverse? Still, the challenge is there: 'It may be said that an emotion is unjustified when a feeling is inappropriate or unfitting to a situation. But I find this unintelligible. Feelings do not have a character that makes this relationship possible.'[12] How feelings might have such a character is a proper and difficult question which we shall eventually have to address. The belief that they cannot, however, draws some support from the other two ostensible deficiencies of emotional feeling.

2. Emotions have the feature of *directedness*. I am angry about your remark, delighted by your discomfiture, surprised at your reaction, contemptuous of the press and so on. Something can cause an emotion via the person's representation of it (for example, of your remark as maliciously intended). Not so with giddiness or lassitude. Feelings such as mellowness, disquiet and tension can occur as blind states. I am not mellow at or about anything; I can be calmed out without being calm about what calms me, as when I am calmed by a tranquilliser. This is especially true of those that border on bodily sensations: I do not itch or ache *at* or *about* anything; and the same goes for tension, release and zip.

   Preliminary caveat: Granting all this, what remains unclear is how wide or narrow is the range of emotional feelings which are blind states. And even if it were all-inclusive, the *aboutness* of emotions would be precluded only if emotions were supposed to consist in feelings and nothing else.

3. However, feelings seem over-primordial in another way that ill-suits them to be essential ingredients of emotions:
   They are so amorphous as to underdetermine the differences between emotions. That is, introspectively there seems little or no difference between the *feeling* a person may have when angry or resentful or indignant. The emotions are distinct, but what distinguishes them are the precise kinds of judgement they involve, not the incensed arousal, the direness, which they share. The same point about a lack of type–type correspondence could be made from the converse direction: different feelings may count as feelings of the same type of emotion under different perceived conditions. Depending on circumstances, *hate* can realise itself, variously, in elation, dejection, anxiousness or spite.

   Preliminary caveat: Ironically, this very inventory of (differentiated) feelings tends to subvert the preceding claim that feelings are introspectively amorphous and lack internal contrasts. Again, the only firm conclusion at this point seems to be that emotions could not always amount exclusively to feelings.

   And it is plain enough that they do not always amount to feelings. For feeling seems episodic, not to say mercurial, in a way that emotion needn't be. Love, hate, fear, jealousy can persist steadily over time while any corresponding states of arousal come and go. I can be angry, even very angry about something depending on what I make of it, whether or not I am ever 'worked up' about it.

In sum, the passion which things can excite in us, the quality and keenness of feeling, can seem a less certain part of our emotions towards them. It is duly relegated by the sort of cognitive approach to emotion that focuses on judgement. It becomes the background noise, not the music.

– Wider Horizons? –

The view that emotions come down to taking certain things to be the case and certain values to be realised could not be correct if either of two things are possible: (1) if an emotion is aroused by the cognitions that also characterise it, that is, if thoughts found an emotion by *causing* it; (2) if emotions can take forms to which the person's thoughts are downright inappropriate. (2) will be considered in Chapters 2–3, so what about (1)?

As thoughts come and go, emotions swell or subside. And it does appear that the thoughts can cause the emotions, even when they also serve as the reasons for them ('Realising how he had taken my remark shocked me out of my complacency and filled me with mortification and regret').

Now, something cannot be its own cause. If having an emotion *consists* in being roused to certain thoughts, it cannot also be roused by them. The thought belonging to the emotion cannot result from itself (or precede itself). For if having a particular emotion *is* (or even entails) being stirred to certain thoughts, they cannot also cause it. For, then, thinking the thoughts would have to cause the person to be aroused by causing him to be aroused by thinking these thoughts. And that is absurd. Causes, as Hume noted, must be logically independent of what they cause.

The beaten path around this sort of dilemma – that either the emotion-founding thoughts are not constitutive of the emotion or they are not its cause – is to point to cases where it is innocuous to describe a thing in terms that include reference to its cause.[13] Consider *burnt*.[14] Here the cause (excessive heat) is understood in the meaning.[15] Presumably, the effect (a blackened, traumatised texture) can be described without reference to the cause. That is because the effect does not actually incorporate the cause here. (Heat remains in a burning substance but not in a burnt one; ashes can be cold.) The problem, however, is that emotions are not just *described* in terms of their causes; we are also supposing that they actually *incorporate* them. To have an emotion is to have the arousing thought (or to be aroused by it). How can there be a constitutive cause?

Perhaps it is actually *frost* that offers the needed analogy. Frost is atmospheric vapour condensed and frozen. A temperature of less than 32° Fahrenheit both precipitates the moisture and, remaining, sustains it in its crystalline form, without which the condensed vapour would be mere dew. In anger, there is a perception of outrage which both calls forth the response and determines its nature: so long, and only so long as this perception lasts, the response is anger (rather than pity or amusement). There would be a problem if all I were galvanised to in anger was an apprehension of outrage; for then if I were also galvanised *by* it, it would be its own cause. Just as there is more to frost than cold (namely, a precipitate of minute ice crystals), so there must be more to anger than just its founding thought if that thought is both to instigate the emotion and to define it. As Jerome Neu puts it, 'even if a thought is a logically necessary or essential constituent of an emotion, it will make sense to say it "causes" the emotion if it causes the *rest* of the emotion, that is i.e. the other constituents'.[16]

The *rest*? The cold that froze the vapour formed crystals, in which the cold persists. Similarly, if thought is to have a causal role, the emotion must have essential properties additional to thought (comparable to the crystalline form of the vapour). If a person's belief is ever to be both cause and ingredient of his emotion, a cognitive conception of emotion must allow that the emotion is richer still. What might its further properties be? Here is a shortlist: physiological changes, desire, preparedness for action, feeling, and, not least, additional cognitions (perhaps other than judgements).

Now, these cannot make equal claims for centrality to the emotions that they may variously characterise. Distinctive physiological changes are sometimes typical of certain emotion types (for example, grief, anger and fear). This does not apply to a particularly broad range of emotions, however; and even where they are typical, they are not necessary, and the identity of the emotional state only occasionally requires their presence (heartfelt grief can be dry-eyed; anger needn't be agitated).[17]

Emotion clearly is a mainspring of *action*. The motivational potency of emotion is more pervasive and obvious. Moreover, there are some stereotypical reactions that can be criterial of certain emotions (starting and exclaiming when startled, raising one's voice when antagonised, blushing and so on). And there are types of action to which particular emotions dispose people (aggression, flight), which may also be criterial of the emotion. Mostly, however, the specific actions and even the types of action to which I will tend when I undergo a certain emotion are not pre-ordained by that emotion alone but depend also on complicated facts about the circumstances, my history, my resources and my other priorities. Moreover, there are important classes of emotion that do not directly move us to act: celebratory emotions (for example, relief or delight) and retrospective emotions such as regret and nostalgia. These, incidentally, are all problems with action-centred theories of emotion, which claim that emotion is a readying of the person to act, or conversely, that it is an inward residue of action which has been inhibited or truncated from the start, or that it is acting but acting magically and in fantasy.[18]

Desire, however, like feeling, seems to have a wider reach across the varieties of emotion. Save in the cases of reflex reactions and other spontaneous stereotypical reactions (such as screaming, recoiling, or smiling), it is *via* awakened desires that emotions create tendencies to act. Even retrospective emotions are characterised by desire (in sorrow I wish things had been different, though no action can realise this, so that there is nothing I directly wish to *do*). However, it might be claimed that desires assimilate to appraisals (value-judgements or other kinds of valuational thought) that help furnish the cognitive basis of an emotion.[19]

The reach of feeling through the emotions seems, if anything, wider: there is hardly a type of emotion of which there *cannot* be feelings. Although it may be true that being angry or afraid does not necessitate having angry feelings or feeling frightened, not even the most zealously parsimonious could deny that there are such things or that they are familiar in cases of anger and fear and not incidental to them. Indeed, a vulnerability to emotional feelings would seem entailed by the *emotion* of anger or fear, for instance, as opposed to the use of the *words* for them to secure rhetorical effect, when a person (or even an organisation) speaks of being 'furious' or 'deeply disappointed' at something simply to stress how unacceptable it is. But it isn't clear, for instance, how desires relate to feelings (whatever the distinction is, in the case of *wistfulness*, for instance, it seems blurred). This only highlights the lack so far of a satisfactory conception of emotional *feeling*. (Is the very notion of it more than an atrophied relic of philosophical Dualism?) Unsurprisingly, then, the relation between thought and these two other ostensible elements of emotion, the urgency (desire) and the keenness (feeling), remains unclear.

Now, further complexity or refinement of cognition has become a widely favoured source for the necessary enrichment. Reservations about feeling noted earlier have only encouraged broadenings of cognitivism. A number of recent cognitive theories of emotion look not only to beliefs and judgements of the obvious kinds but beyond. Thus, an emotion might involve compounded thoughts, not all of which are its causes. A recognition ('that snake is poisonous') may elicit and justify a given *type* of emotional response with value-judgements filling out its more precise content ('How appalling'/'How exciting'). Again, non-assertional kinds of thought, such as picturings, that do not amount to belief, may supervene on outright beliefs, or even cut across them; or they may replace judgement altogether (for example, as perhaps they do in our responses to fiction). Yet another step is to seek emotion in the hedonic loading of thoughts, judgemental or non-judgemental.

One purpose of these latter ideas is to do justice to the affective aspects of emotion, to emotive feeling, in broadly cognitive terms. If an analysis of emotion in terms of beliefs fails to do this, invoking the need for a theory of feeling, then non-assertional thoughts and hedonic loading will come into their own to offer a comprehensive, and comprehensively cognitive, conception of the emotions. This is an ambitious prospect and for many a reassuring one.

What we must ask, then, is how far the resources of belief and judgement stretch and how far the more venturesome recent cognitive theories can extend these. Beyond waits the question whether cognitivism in any form suffices to illuminate affect without help from a quite different perspective.

– NOTES –

1. Hume (1955), p. 415.
2. Ibid., p. 458.
3. Belief and judgement differ in that a person may acquire a belief more passively than by passing judgement on the matter; but since a belief is presumably something a person *would* affirm, beliefs may be seen as dispositional judgements. Where the difference is unimportant, I shall use the terms interchangeably.
4. Bedford (1956), p. 109. Judgemental cognitivism became an almost standard view in the philosophy of emotion and, in a variety of forms, remains influential. Prominent examples of it include: Nussbaum (1993), chapter 10; Solomon (1993), chapters 8 and 10; Gordon (1987); Davidson (1980b); Lyons (1980), chapters 2 and 4; Neu (1977); Trigg (1970); Hampshire (1965), pp. 84, 97; Pitcher (1965); Kenny (1963), chapter III; see also Ben-Ze'ev (1997). Philosophers unhappy with judgemental cognitivism still labour to exorcise it (see, for instance, Madell (1996) and Ridley (1997)).
5. Elster (1989), p. 64.
6. According to Robert Gordon (1987), the recognition of what anger, for instance, purports to be about must be the cause of anger or the person in question is not really

subject to anger: 'Cognitions of the sort I am discussing seem to be required not just for "normal" or "appropriate" anger but for the label angry to be applicable at all' (p. 56; see also pp. 22 and 60). An emotion is downright precluded by the failure of its cognitive conditions.

7. Bedford (1956), p. 116.
8. Ibid., p. 119.
9. Solomon (1993), pp. 185–6.
10. Zajonc (1980), pp. 152–3.
11. Pitcher (1965), p. 330.
12. Bedford (1956), p. 121.
13. See, for instance, Donald Davidson's classic (1980a), p. 13ff.
14. The ensuing discussion is indebted to Aaron Ridley and Alex Neill (1991), pp. 106–8.
15. See Green (1972), p. 38; and Wilson (1972), pp. 25–6.
16. Neu (1977), p. 161.
17. The deeper physiology of all emotion, each emotion's cortico-limbic story, is hardly ever, if at all, part of what is *understood* by the type of emotion in question.
18. As proposed, respectively, by Thalberg (1977), Hampshire (1976) and Sartre (1962).
19. The claim that desire constitutes the dynamic element in emotion does need further consideration, which it receives in Chapter 3.

CHAPTER 2

Emotions that Confound Thought

A woman is the only thing I am afraid of that I know won't hurt
me.

Abraham Lincoln

– FIRST IMPRESSIONS –

One of the arresting things about being human is the waywardness of
emotions. Even my own are not always expected, or what I would expect.
They may take forms for which my beliefs have not prepared me. That
is, the congruence of an emotion with the kinds of thought that ought
to make for it can be strained. This dissonance is at its most radical when
emotion occurs irrationally. In one or another shape, this is a familiar
experience. Emotions are notorious for it. Yet what it is is not so easily
determined as some writers have presumed, and its lessons concerning
the nature of emotion (particularly the role of belief and other kinds of
cognition in it) are hard to weigh.

What actually makes an emotion irrational? Groundless fears and
uncalled-for anger spring to mind. One way these can arise is for the
beliefs appropriate to the sort of emotion in question to be mistaken in
the particular case at hand. The emotion is consonant with the person's
judgements, but these are mistaken – or if true, they are true by accident,
as when a hypochondriac's worst fears are, unbeknownst to him, actually
borne out. Of course, not just any mistake will do. A simple medieval
sailor's fear of plunging over the edge of the world is not irrational. For
this, avoidance of the error must be within the person's grasp. The person's
evidence is inadequate or he has misconstrued it (Othello's jealousy, for
instance, involves both), and it lies in his power to realise this. Typically,
he has passed judgement impulsively, without bothering to weigh the
available reasons. Often his mind turns in a vicious circle: he would not
form the ill-judged beliefs if he wasn't subject to the emotion. Such a
person is deceived, misguided or confused. Were he clearer, better
informed or more circumspect, he would think differently and therefore

react differently. Since the link between his emotion and the relevant beliefs is untroubled – is the same as in non-irrational cases – cognitive theories of emotion have nothing to fear from irrationality of this kind.[1] And cognitive steps towards improved understanding are promising remedies for it. The truth can make him free.

However, this is not the only form taken by irrational emotion. Cases of a more recalcitrant kind are all too frequent. The beliefs a person holds which are relevant to the type of emotion he has can be in line with the truth or with the evidence available to him or with what anyone would or should think, and yet be out of line with his emotion. He doesn't think the house is haunted – he doesn't believe in ghosts at all – yet he is terrified to enter that house and certainly unable to spend a night there. It is not unknown for a newly bereaved widow to find herself prey to anger and bitterness at her husband for having 'left' her even though she knows full well that his death was not by choice, much less 'aimed' at her. It might be contended that the bereaved woman's anger at her husband for having abandoned her just does imply (and reveal) a belief that the death was indeed an act of abandonment. Certainly, expressing the anger as anger at this 'act', at being forsaken, is a way of bringing into relief how she feels, namely forsaken. Yet just as it would be wrong to infer what these locutions on their own imply, that the husband died by way of leaving her, so it would be wrong to infer from her saying she is angry at him for deserting her that she really believes this to be the true account of what he has done (or that he has *done* anything). It would be perfectly intelligible for someone distressed in this way and asked the question straight, 'Do you really think he did it deliberately – that he intended to spite you by dying?', to reply, 'I suppose not. When it comes down to it I realise that's silly, but somehow I just do feel bitter.' Young children confronted with the divorce of their parents sometimes openly and without apparent reason blame themselves for what is happening, and there is no reason to doubt that this is indeed just what they think when they say it. But a distraught adult is not a distraught child, and similar assumptions cannot be made with confidence (failing special reasons for doing so, an issue we shall consider in due course). The possibility that would be expressed by the bereaved woman's answer, 'I know he didn't really', is distinct from two others: (1) akratic belief, where a person confesses to a belief she simultaneously acknowledges to be unfounded; or (2) downright delusion, where a false belief is held without any thought of its credentials. However, a person who feels bitter in bereavement need not be downright delusional or even hold the beliefs that make sense of the attitude of reproach. Thus,

> The death of a young person frequently elicits an unusual outpouring of grief. Brown recalls the time when a mother hit her dead son during a wake. 'I guess because she was so mad that he had gotten killed. She kept yelling "You didn't listen to me and look at what happened."'[2]

Must she suppose the boy is listening now?

Now, what can the structure of a person's mind be when they respond in such a way? In the earlier sort of example, in which the emotion is consonant with the beliefs but these are not consonant with the world, the fault is cognitive and the person is necessarily unaware of it. Once he recognises how his beliefs are at fault the irrationality will rectify itself and the emotion will transform. By contrast, in the second sort of case the person can be perfectly aware of the fault, aware that he 'knows better' than to have the emotion he is having, without thereby dissipating or altering the emotion. Overtly phobic cases are the simplest examples: 'Phobic patients usually recognise that their fear is excessive and unrealistic' and 'in controlled trials of psychotherapy phobias have not shown impressive change despite discussion and working through the origins of the phobias'.[3] The skewed relation here is between emotion and belief and resides, so to speak, within the person. This is in contrast to the mismatch of belief and world, so we may speak here of 'internal' or 'subjective' irrationality as distinct from 'objective' irrationality (the former type of case).

Now it *is* puzzling how I could find a deserted house frightening whilst really believing there is nothing about it to fear. And it is not always obvious whether or when this is happening. Reactions can seem more irrational than they are. There is more than one way of regarding something as dangerous or to be feared, for instance. Maybe the danger is indefinite: the person is led to think he doesn't think there is any danger because he can't identify quite what the danger he senses is – *why* the situation seems ominous – but however elusive it may be he does believe *a* danger to be there, something unspecified and lurking. Or perhaps the sort of danger is well understood but its presence is uncertain. He is making Pascal's Wager. Though he doesn't think the danger is at hand, he does think it could be, and better safe than sorry. He really doesn't think the house is haunted or, more generally, that the 'living dead' live, but how sure is he? Fear *of* can be fear *lest* as well as fear *that*.

Not all putative cases of subjective irrationality can be explained away so easily. Always to foist the appropriate beliefs on to the victim of perverse emotion can be to overlook some of the beliefs he actually has. Certainly, thinking something *may* be dangerous can, by a kind of auto-suggestion, predispose one to think it *is* dangerous, other things being equal.[4] But in cases of subjective irrationality other things are not equal. There, the belief the person explicitly and unequivocally has (or lacks, as the case may be) actually precludes the belief that would make sense of the type of emotion that assails him. In the example of the house, not only does the person believe the house is not haunted, he also does not believe the house is haunted. So it is not just a case of holding recognised inconsistent beliefs (if that is possible). Such a person, when frightened, denies, without also affirming, that the house is haunted; and he denies it in addition to also affirming that the house is not haunted. So the belief his fear needs is missing. His emotion flourishes despite all he believes rather than because of something he believes.

– Two Kinds of Irrationality? –

Is the foregoing too clear-cut a picture of the beliefs in phobias and the like? Can emotions really part company with them to the extent suggested?

Knowing one's own mind is harder than it looks. One's thoughts may disclose themselves only obliquely. And emotion can be a way of involuntarily and unwittingly laying bare what one really thinks. Just as one emotion can be diagnostic of another (for example, disappointment of hope), so can it be indicative of a thought. Pride or shame indicate a connection I take myself to have and a value I put on what I suppose myself connected with. On a representational understanding of emotion, of course, that is what we should invariably expect. This makes what seem to be flagrantly ill-grounded emotions, such as phobias and other 'silly' or bizarre fears and delights, into test-cases. And so we must consider rather carefully whether they may not tell us more about what the person thinks than he can.

A simple and inviting way of attempting to preserve a suitable judgemental component within what I have presented as subjectively irrational emotions, would be to suppose a sharp general distinction between factual and evaluative judgements and beliefs. This would consort nicely with stress on the centrality of value-judgements to emotions found in some current philosophy (as, for instance, in Martha Nussbaum's *Therapy of*

Desire). The position might then be that the person in question does make the value-judgement proper to the type of emotion he has but does not hold the factual beliefs appropriate to this value-judgement. Thus, if *appalling* is a valuational term and *destructive* is merely factual, a phobic person might be held to deem appalling what he does not suppose destructive. The irrationality would consist in the failure of his factual beliefs to provide sufficient grounding for his appraisal.

Unfortunately this sort of account mislocates the clash. Irrational emotion can befall even a person whose judgements are all in perfect harmony. Recognising perfectly that feathers or open spaces have no destructive powers, a phobic person may also hold them innocent and yet find them appalling. A bereaved person may well regard as a pity the very loss he can't seem to grieve over; he thinks he should grieve because he thinks it is a pity and sad, not just because he thought it would be. And this failure of his emotion to live up to his appraisals, particular as well as general, is precisely what makes the lack of emotion so disconcerting and so puzzling to him.

– Elusive Cognition: Deeper Resources –

There are subtler ways in which what appear to be internally irrational emotions might still be shadows cast by thought. Thoughts can elude their thinker in several ways. One may hold beliefs without realising it, beliefs one doesn't avow or think of oneself as accepting. Perhaps, too, beliefs which one would sincerely disavow can be held all the same, unconsciously. Again, one may be affected by a picture of something that does not amount to a belief about it. In any or all of these ways a view of something can insinuate itself without being a matter of outright judgement. Can one or another of these possibilities be relied on to account for cases of apparent discrepancy between a person's emotion and what he accepts and rejects?

– Tacit Belief –

Where I have an emotion without the basis it needs in what I judge true, one way of making sense of this would be by interpreting me as believing the right things for someone with my reactions but as believing them covertly. They are things that are true to me without my realising this. My emotion may uniquely signal a *disposition*, an otherwise unrecognised readiness, to believe. As such, emotion offers an instrument of self-exploration and discovery, revealing of the more obscure or neglected byways of personal commitment. In fact, on the harder cognitive conception of emotion, in which having certain beliefs is a condition of a response *counting* as an instance of a given emotion, either I must have the right belief somehow or I have actually misconstrued my reaction. And once more, my apparent emotional response is a vehicle of self-discovery. Consider first an action. Suppose I balk at placing trust in a friend on an important matter even though this inconveniences me and causes embarrassment or worse. I might surprise myself by this reluctance. There is a natural interpretation of such an act: when the chips are down, I do not regard this friend as trustworthy. This may never have occurred to me, and I may try to avoid admitting it and seek to rationalise my choice in some other way.

Is it not similar with emotions? I find myself angry with a friend, annoyed by whatever he says or does, prone to flare up at the slightest pretext. But I realise this and it puzzles me; I wonder what has come over me. Again, one response is to interpret me as believing something about him that I don't realise (and wouldn't like to think) I believe about him. It might, for instance, be that I regarded a remark he made as condescending and hence as disclosing a lack of respect.

The question is, when are interpretations of this form justified and what justifies them? Tracing tacit beliefs presents problems. In the first place, the mere fact that what I do or how I respond accords with a certain proposition does not imply that I believe this proposition. And this is true even where what I do or how I react is invariably consistent with the proposition. A cyclist rides unthinkingly. He has never plumbed the secret of his riding skill and so he cannot be harbouring it. That secret, the formula he follows without knowing it, apparently, is this:

> When he starts falling to the right he turns the handlebars towards the right, so that the course of the bicycle is deflected along a curve towards the right. This results in a centrifugal force pushing the cyclist to the left and offsets the gravitational force dragging him down to the right. This manoeuvre presently throws the cyclist out of balance to the left, which he counteracts by turning the handlebars to the left; and so he continues to keep himself in balance by winding along a series of appropriate curvatures. A simple analysis shows that for a given angle of unbalance the curvature of each winding is inversely proportional to the square of the speed at which the cyclist is proceeding.[5]

Mere systematic consistency with my responses, behaviour and so on is clearly not sufficient to rank something as an unexplicit belief of mine or as something I (don't know that I) know.

One criterion for tacit beliefs that improves on mere consistency is directness of implication: the things I unwittingly believe are the immediate logical consequences of the beliefs I do avow, even if these things haven't occurred to me. My present beliefs place them ready to hand, obvious rather than entombed in labyrinths of logical intricacy.

A general difficulty with this is that even the elementary logical baggage of my judgements is vast, if mostly trivial, and there may be connections that just haven't occurred to me, however simple they are, and which if they did occur to me would amount to discoveries, not things I would say I had supposed all along.[6] As I arrange over the phone to meet you in half an hour's time I do presume (tacitly believe) that you are alive and not too far away to reach our meeting point in that time. But do I further accept that you are not in Australia (as I might if I knew you had just made a trip there) or that you are neither in Australia, Burundi, Irkutsk and every other specific place in the world that isn't hereabouts? On the other hand, I may tacitly believe things that are not *logical* consequences of anything I explicitly believe, such as that the Apollo 11 mission wasn't faked.[7] In no sense do I *believe* either all the logical consequences of what I explicitly believe or all that I do not disbelieve.

However, even if there were no uncertainties about whether direct implication fixes tacit belief, it would avail little as applied to renegade emotions. For the belief that needs to underlie the dread of a reputedly haunted house is the belief that the house actually is or might be haunted (or, at one step further removed, that ghosts exist or are possible); and this is anything but a direct consequence of what I undoubtedly do (explicitly) believe, namely that these things are certainly false. Nor does it cohere, at further remove, with my materialist cosmology. Indeed, it is precisely the *logical* anomaly of the required belief in relation to my other beliefs which generates the *psychological* anomaly of the emotion, that is, the strangeness of my dread.[8]

Perhaps, then, the criterion of tacit belief lies more in the psychological than the logical relation of the believer and what he is supposed to believe. This approach circumscribes the range of candidates for tacit belief more realistically. Here, I am supposed to believe tacitly what I may not avow explicitly but would assent to under certain conditions. The problem here is to find conditions of assent that distinguish tacit believing from forms of readiness to believe that are just states of not yet believing (being prepared to judge someone guilty given just one more piece of evidence does not qualify as tacit belief in guilt). The most obvious qualifying condition would be reflection, what I would assent to upon considering the matter. Again, though, it is unclear how this differs from coming to believe. However much the reflection condition might be refined, the very idea of being disposed to believe (even being on the edge of believing) seems to imply that the believing remains unprecipitated.[9] A glass that is fragile is a glass that has yet to shatter.

Once more, whatever the general merits of this approach, it would not yield tacit beliefs that could sustain deviant emotions. For in too many cases, their host has reflected on the issue (or can reflect on it) *without* acknowledging the belief in question – or any disposition to it, for that matter.

So far, the reasonable suspicion that renegade emotions signal unvoiced layers of belief is not borne out. What makes this idea tempting in the first place? Suppose there *is* a strong link between what people think and what they are actually prepared (or not prepared) to *do* – that actions speak louder than words when it comes to settling what one really regards as true and as best. Given this deep connection, then wherever preference follows emotion, the person's thoughts must be such as to make sense of the person's preferences. The demands of practical rationality would demand cognitive rectitude in emotions – and a suitable cognitive core to emotion. Now, our preferences, given their head, do indeed tend to harmonise with our 'senseless' passions. Where nothing much else is at stake, I am content to shun the phobic object, happy to shrink from throwing knives at my mother's portrait (that I know isn't her) or to try with desperation to retrieve the lost wedding ring (that I know isn't my marriage).

The assumption that what a person (who is free and sane) prefers is a matter of what he thinks – of what he thinks true and what he thinks best – is, however, unsafe. In the case of emotions, it is not clear that this direct connection holds. The fact that an emotion is not, as one realises, well founded is not by itself a reason to resist the choices to which it inclines one. Even if I do not believe that the picture of my mother is my mother, *that* is no reason why I should aspire to be able to throw knives at it with equanimity. In 'Remarks on Frazer's *Golden Bough*', Wittgenstein draws attention to a rite of adoption in which the prospective mother passes the child down through her clothing and out between her legs.[10] Of course, the adoptive mother in Frazer's account need not suppose at any level that she is giving birth to the baby she passes down through her clothing in order to have reason to perform the ritual. The ritual needn't leave her believing she is the child's natural mother any more than it finds her believing that. It is not her *belief* that she is acting on. Of course, she would have no reason to perform this ritual if it was irrelevant to making her the child's mother. But it isn't as though the only way the ritual act can contribute to making her the child's mother is by inducing her to believe this event to be the child's birth. Presumably the whole point of the ritual is to confer motherhood on a woman who has not borne the child herself.

This is not to say that the resemblance between the adoptive mother's act and childbearing is accidental, any more than placing a ring on someone's finger or having intercourse with them is accidental as a way of sealing a bond. Suggestiveness accrues to a ritual act by what it contrives to resemble. This suggestiveness can dispose the one who performs it to some of the same emotion that could be evoked by what it resembles. The form of the adoption ceremony might tap the special affection for a child with whom there is a unique and physical tie that transcends affection for children generally. The woman could be made to feel a mother, as distinct from made to think she is one. The dart-thrower risks some of the horror and guilt that committing an actual physical assault on his mother would stir. The suggestion respectively of giving birth and matricide serves rather to arouse than to persuade, and to arouse by symbolising. This can be effected causally without being achieved rationally. Here, emotion develops without its usual reliance on thought. This is just as well, since emotions may be desirable where the relevant beliefs are not available (as in the case of the adoptive mother).

Where not having a particular belief is not a reason for desisting from a certain practice, embracing the practice isn't a reason for postulating the belief.

In whatever way tacit belief is to be understood, it is hard to see how I could at all believe anything I explicitly *dis*believe; and with wayward emotions, this is apt to include the beliefs that would underwrite them.

– Unconscious belief –

Tacit beliefs are susceptible to recognition and acknowledgement. The belief which would properly underlie a renegade emotion is likely to be disclaimed, however. But there is a well-trodden path from this to the presumption that it must be a belief which is *inaccessible* to recognition and acknowledgement. Maybe ordinary reflection cannot plumb all of what a person believes. Perhaps the mind passes some of its judgements *in camera*. Thus, the person actually does accept the judgements proper to the emotion. He accepts them either instead of or in addition to the judgements he sincerely espouses which are adverse to the emotion, but he accepts them *unconsciously*. Thus,

> Much of psychoanalysis seems underpinned by the idea that between any person's emotions or affects and their causal objects or causes there obtains a real appropriateness or actual proportionality no matter how discrepant or incongruous those relations may seem and regardless of the person's mental condition . . . Freud's psychoanalytic interpretations of incongruities of affect *always* try to show that the incongruities are only ostensible. They try, that is, to disclose an actual congruity, a real appropriateness, behind what is taken to be the facade of every apparently discrepant feeling.[11]

As David Sachs puts it, 'a person's thoughts or beliefs often have effects upon him, among which effects are affects'. [12]

It would be rash to exclude the possibility that, when someone is subject to perplexing emotions, the reason may lie in a perception of things that he has but is unable to acknowledge, and to which his present emotional vulnerabilities are a clue.

However, there is room to question whether such a diagnosis in terms of unconsciously held beliefs (or fantasies) is the only possibility. The unconscious is an easily evoked *deus ex machina*, but the burden of proof would seem to rest on anyone who presumes that nothing else could be said about the examples we are considering.

And there are reasons why caution is advisable about this and why room should be allowed for the sort of alternative that I have suggested, namely genuine internal irrationality. The first problem with exclusive reliance on the hypothesis of unconscious belief is simply that there may be no reason to accept it. If no amount of hindsight – of reflection and subsequent experience – disposes this person to change his mind about what he thought at the time,[13] the claim that different and unconscious judgements must have been at work would rank as dogmatic, as an ad hoc hypothesis on the part of a psychoanalytically minded cognitivism. Admittedly, there is the possibility that in all (and certainly in some) such cases, the person just cannot grasp what the true state of his thoughts was at the time. To deny that this could happen would be no less dogmatic than to insist that it always must.

However, there are additional reasons for hesitating to accord all the cases in question a basis in unconscious belief. In the case of at least some apparently incongruous emotions, phobias, we saw that available evidence weighs against this approach (other evidence to similar effect is reviewed in the Appendix to this chapter). Perhaps this is just as well in view of the difficulty of even imagining what some of these beliefs could be.

Indeed, the whole idea of unconscious belief, judgings in one's heart of hearts, presents problems. What can justify belief in unconscious beliefs? The difficulty with this can be appreciated if we combine two facts noticed in connection with tacit belief: the fact that acting and reacting as one who believed a proposition *p* is an insufficient reason for ascribing this belief, and the fact that the mind of someone prey to a renegade emotion is not actually organised altogether consistently with the postulated belief. And if the person does eventually assent to *p* (for example, in the course of analysis), the question again arises as to what shows the person isn't coming to this belief at the time of assenting to it. What shows this newly found assent to be the person's discovery about his antecedent state of mind as distinct from a step in forming a salutary narrative about himself? Some would say that edifying narratives are all one can hope to achieve. But that precisely challenges the idea of diagnosis founded on fact.[14] This would make criteria such as explanatory economy loom larger in the framing of the personal narrative; so that if there are more parsimonious accounts than the one psychoanalysis encourages, they must be taken seriously.

Furthermore, perhaps what 'unconscious' mental states are would itself be clarified by knowing which roles they don't play. So it seems prudent to explore the consequences of forswearing blanket appeal to unconscious beliefs here. Occam's razor can teach.

It should be clear by now that beliefs have a surprising potential for unobvious kinds of lodgement but equally that what looks like irrationality in emotions is not a manifestation of elusive and unexpected beliefs.

– Beyond Belief –

And yet, irrationality could still trace to dissonant cognitions. Perhaps the *cognitive* background to perverse emotions involves more than beliefs and judgements. Thus, in trying to understand apparent conflicts of heart with head, the picture of rival judgements, one ostensible and the other not, might be replaced with a different picture, now of a conflict between thoughts of divergent kinds as well as contrasting contents. Someone could think of Dunkirk as a victory without thinking that it was a victory. Thought is multiform. It can be assertional (as in judgements and beliefs) or non-assertional. In the first case, a thought concerning something involves accepting as true a proposition about it; in the second it is a matter of a proposition seeming to be true of the object whether or not one actually accepts its truth. The latter is analogous to (and sometimes identical with) the aspectual dimension of sense perception: seeing the drawing of the Necker cube as three-dimensional doesn't require believing it so. The distinction is between what one thinks *x* is and how one thinks of it (what it *appears* to one as being). I can wonder whether something is as menacing as it looks. I can be wise to my fantasies (of omnipotence or victimhood). The characterisation of something in a certain light needn't be underwritten by belief.

Portrayal usually reflects belief, but the two can diverge. The lines in the Muller–Lyer figure strike me as unequal, and I will accept this if I don't know about the illusion; whilst if I do know, the lines will still *seem* unequal even if I *accept* that they are equal. A certain picture of things can impress itself on me whether I am convinced by it or not. Robert Roberts calls thoughts of this kind, 'construals'.[15]

Many emotions are undoubtedly founded on construals of their objects that fall short of outright judgements, and a number of philosophers see in them the best hope for a cognitive theory of the emotions. Later we will consider their role more fully (in Chapters 5 and 8). Here the question is whether this approach sweeps up the cases in which a person's emotion ill-suits his ostensible beliefs.

The way in which it could claim to do this is clear enough: My construal of something is at odds with what I actually believe about it. The old house has an eerie and ominous character to me and I can't help thinking of ghosts in it (hence my fear of it), but of course I *suppose* no such thing (hence the irrationality of my fear).

I suggest that at most this advances our understanding of how emotions can be irrational without completing it. And in fact, I think it subtly misdescribes the instances of these emotions presented above. First, a general observation. There are two backgrounds against which I may fail to believe a proposition: (1) I don't believe *p* is true (I disbelieve it). Here, I am prepared to entertain the conceivability of *p*'s truth and do so in rejecting *p* as false. (2) I don't believe *p*, but neither do I disbelieve it. I fail to believe it not in the way that I fail to believe Oswald alone killed Kennedy but in the way I fail to believe in ghosts, magic, the Greek gods or illusoriness of the external world. Namely, the very question of *p*'s truth doesn't arise for me, hasn't occurred to me and wouldn't be entertained as a possibility. *P*'s truth cannot be accommodated in a world-order that I can understand.

Now, in (1) I can think of *p* as true even though I accept that it isn't.

In (2) I can't think of p as true – *that p* could never be more than something fanciful, like the events in a fairy-tale. Accordingly, the irrational scruples of two people each of whom is unnerved at the prospect of entering a lonely, tumble-down house conceal an important difference if the first person accepts that this place is not haunted but regards haunting generally as a possibility whilst to the second the very idea of investment by spirits is out of the question and thus not even a risk. The second person cannot and does not even think of the house as being haunted; the first can and presumably does think of it (construe it) in this way. To require of the second person that it can at least *seem* to him as a house that is haunted, that he see it as haunted, is actually incorrect. Seeing it as spooky needn't mean seeing it as spoo*ked*.

Of course, the idea of supernatural presence can play a part in his response to the house, but its role is best appreciated by considering the way in which it would be most natural to express this person's vantage-point: he does *feel* as he would if the house did seem haunted to him. For this to be so, it may not be necessary to assume that it even *seems* haunted to him, that he actually sees or construes it under this aspect.

Consider now a phobia which actually does include the construal. Would the construal offer a cognitive key to the skewed fear? One can make pictures of something (images or fantasies) that do not correspond to one's beliefs about it, and this does offer a way in which one can think against one's better judgement. So is that what is happening in seemingly renegade emotions?

Well, presumably, the construal must have an intelligible content, for it is supposed to make sense of the phobia, which lacks sense in relation to what the person believes. That feathers (or something about them, like their sheen) are 'ghastly' or that brown is 'excruciating' cannot then be ways of construing them, because they are already the voices of phobia itself, not its foundation. Certainly, phobic fear of feathers is *like* the fear of something as a threat, but it needn't *be* fear of them in these terms (or perhaps in any other terms). For if the awfulness of feathers is alleged to lie in how they are like a dense carpet of layered blades, the problem is that this construal does not carry the terror with it, since it is quite possible to understand or summon the construal without being possessed with terror. Just as between the screech of fingernails raking a blackboard and the excruciating unbearableness of this sound to some people, there is no descriptive bridge that makes the reaction seem natural or inevitable to those not already susceptible to it (to whatever degree). The shudder is not the sound, however described. On the other hand, the descriptions that really are evocative of it (the *hideousness* or *frightfulness* of the feathers) are expressive rather than explanatory. And this applies just as much to construals as it does to judgements.

Consider snakes. Someone can be leery of snakes as such, even the innocuous ones, without being downright phobic about them. Here the *belief* with regard to harmless snakes is that they are harmless. Yet how they *seem* (are construed) is: sinister. The emotion, leeriness, may contrast clearly with the full horror released by some other, truly phobic object. The mild (but still 'silly') aversion here does not attain the necessary ferocity and grip on the will. This means that the person who *is* phobic about all snakes may indeed construe them as sinister, but it doesn't follow that his construal accounts for their negative magnetism, their fully phobic aura. Is it a matter, then, of *how* sinister they seem? This does not seem anything other than how *fearsomely* sinister they appear. And that may be hard to specify save in terms of their power, as snakes, to horrify him. There may be nothing further about his actual vision of them than just that they are sinister. But, again that perceived quality does not guarantee phobia.

Seeing aspects and changes to them can be voluntary. So a construal of snakes as sinister may amount to this: I can appreciate how snakes could look sinister, although I don't have to see them in this way and could see them differently. But phobia does not lend itself to being shifted out of in this way. Furthermore, even if a therapy did work by laboriously weaning me of my dread vision of snakes, that could be because this vision was a *sine qua non* of horror at snakes, not sufficient or tantamount to it.

With some quite familiar aversions, it is hard to locate any type of thought, even a construal. For irreligious and unsuperstitious people to shrink from corpses, as they are apt to, need not be for them to be prey to any thoughts (however surreptitious and renegade) of supernatural danger. But there is nothing gratuitous or theoretical about the dread that corpses can inspire in such people. The emotion is unmistakably there, even where the right thought is not.[16]

Wayward emotions such as phobic fear reveal that some emotions, at least, can occur independently of the sorts of thought that could give them grounds, and this includes non-assertional thought. They can arise even in the teeth of thoughts that should preclude them. This fact suggests that while having the right thoughts may be typical of a given type of emotion and even necessary to distinguishing it as a type from other types, it is not always necessary in individual instances. Nor, therefore, can it be necessary to the identification of the emotion in these individual cases or to its composition. – That is the probing conclusion to which the discussion so far seems to point.

– ARE IRRATIONAL EMOTIONS EXCEPTIONS THAT PROVE THE RULE? –

Is this sweeping inference justified? It may be asked how seriously this kind of case should be taken when trying to understand what emotions are. In the first place, it is unclear how far one can generalise from one sort of example. How many emotions offer counterparts to phobias, that is, can occur, often with extreme force in gross detachment from their proprietary reasons? Can sane people find themselves admiring things they genuinely find mediocre or detestable? – One could multiply the examples of emotions that do not seem susceptible to subjective irrationality. Some emotions, indeed, are constitutionally incapable of fitting the formula for subjective irrationality. I could not *envy* myself (*especially* if I regard my lot as enviable!),[17] nor could I envy another for something which I would never wish for myself even in a fit of masochism.

On the other hand, not only fear but depression, elation, anger, hatred, delectation and fascination, to name but a few, arguably can fit the formula for subjective irrationality.

Still, it may be asked how much these wayward occurrences of given emotions can reveal about the standard, *non*-wayward occurrences of them. Do patently disordered emotional phenomena such as phobias teach us anything about emotions in their normal forms? Hard cases make bad law; perhaps misbegotten passions are mere curiosities.

Several things should dispel this misgiving. Ill-formed thoughts (for example, incomplete or self-contradictory) are not thoughts at all. They are abortive. Not so with renegade emotions, they are perfectly real instances of their well-constituted types. Phobic fear may be exceptional and is cognitively perverse, but there is no doubt that as fear it is the real article. Neither is renegade emotion always pathological, that is, worthless and in need of being dispelled or coaxed into a more reasonable form. Nor is it uncommon, nor inconsequential. It therefore merits exploration in its own right. What, if anything, it has to teach about emotion generally will then be easier to see.

Consider, as just one example, the susceptibility to feeling personal guilt in the manifest absence of personal culpability. Guilt incurred (or even imputed) collectively can be received personally, even though the recognised prerequisite of individual guilt (that is, personal responsibility for what incurred the guilt) is plainly not met.

Oblique guilt of this kind is not like a nasty taste or even phobic fear. A core of belief clearly survives at its heart: 'We are implicated and (thus) I am implicated.' Moreover, the nature of this thought is what distinguishes the response of guilt from one of shame. A response of shame (also possible here) would impute a loss of honour rather than a failed responsibility (though the latter could be a ground for the former). And so shame would not be irrational here in the same way guilt is (for guilt needs responsibility). But then, shame may be less rational by its very nature. For what can actually *justify* honour by association (perhaps very tangential association at that)? Those who are all too susceptible to shame may be at a loss for any judgement or perception that would justify or even explain some of the very potent dependence that honour has on association. And even though guilt-at-a-distance retains a rickety judgemental basis and so is not the purest form of subjective irrationality, it too rests ultimately on sand. Could a hundred Jesuits furnish the innocent citizen with *reason* why he should feel stained by the crimes of others? And mightn't a moment's reflection on this fact disabuse the citizen even of the fragile perception of being 'somehow' implicated? Then all that would remain is the kind of feeling that he or she has when they *do* take themselves to have failed a responsibility. Yet while a personal sharing in collective guilt may be without any ground that the person could find (as that of a repentant perpetrator would be), it is not a misbegotten and wasted emotion, as is a phobia. A conscience that was not to be stirred by intimations of collective responsibility ('Sure, it's a pity, but what has it got to do with *me?*') would be the less for that. Perhaps personal receptivity to collective guilt received personally is admirable because it testifies to a general moral vigilance and generosity that can only be welcomed. This might also have a utility value: a tendency in individuals to identify with present or past acts of the polities they belong to could serve to inhibit repeated crimes of Us against Them. So there may be reason for this personal response even if there isn't reason in it.

Nevertheless, it remains a kind of benign moral illusion, for here, there is nothing of which the person is really guilty. Because the appropriateness of collective guilt does not rest on moral fact, the pinning of collective guilt on the individual is acceptable on the part of the acknowledger, but not from anyone else. Although it is seemly for the individual himself to respond as if implicated, it is distinctly unseemly for those on the outside so to respond. He transgresses if he feels uninvolved; they transgress if they involve him.

In sum, some emotions are capable of genuinely deviating from the cognitive orientation, however it is constructed, of the person affected by them at the time. This phenomenon is neither unfamiliar or necessarily pathological. Such responses can serve us well:

> In spite of herself, Ursula felt herself recoiling from Hermione. It was all she could do to restrain her revulsion . . . She ran home plunged in thought . . . There was a sort of league between the two women. And yet she could not bear her. But she put the thought away. 'She's really good,' she said to herself.[18]

They are also instructive: emotions needn't echo their host's thoughts and so cannot entail them.

– APPENDIX –
EMOTIONS AND THEIR COGNITIVE FOUNDATIONS: SOME PSYCHOLOGICAL PERSPECTIVES

The idea that cognition is essential to emotion has been well represented in experimental psychology: 'cognitive appraisal (of meaning and significance) underlies and is an integral feature of all emotional states. Are there any exceptions? I think not'.[19]

However, starting with a noted paper called 'Feeling and Thinking: Preferences need no Inferences', R. B. Zajonc has sought to rehabilitate Wilhelm Wundt's claim of long ago that,

> When any physical process rises above the threshold of consciousness, it is the affective elements ('Gefuhlselemente') which as soon as they are strong enough, first become noticeable . . . They are sometimes states of pleasurable or unpleasurable character, sometimes they are predominantly states of strained expectation. Often there is vividly present the special affective tone of the forgotten idea, although the idea itself still remains in the background of consciousness. In a similar manner the clear apperception of ideas in acts of cognition and recognition is always preceded by feelings.[20]

Among the evidence that Zajonc adduces for this kind of claim is work on perception according to which 'the first level of response to the environment is affective. The direct emotional impact of the situation, perhaps largely a global response to the ambience, very generally governs the direction taken by subsequent relations with the environment.' And this can actually prefigure the course that cognition itself will take: 'It sets the motivational tone and delimits the kinds of experiences that one expects and seeks.'[21]

Can something unrecognised elicit an emotional response? Surely 'A creature that is oblivious to the significance of what is happening for its well-being does not react with an emotion.'[22] There are at least two persuasive pieces of evidence that this is indeed possible.

In one, random sequences of tunes were presented repeatedly to one ear while a story was read in the subject's other ear. Although the subject could not avoid hearing the tunes, he was made to concentrate instead on the story, the text of which he had to follow and confirm that it matched what he was hearing. The subjects were then given a recognition test in which the tunes they had heard were mixed with tunes not heard before. They were also asked to classify all these tunes according to how much they liked them. Some did the recognition test first, some the liking rating. The result was that success in recognising the tunes previously heard repeatedly was little better than chance, and yet these tunes were reported *liked* more often than the new tunes. Liking was a marked function of what had been heard, but these tunes could not be identified as heard previously. It seems, in Zajonc's words, that 'There is a strong path from stimulus exposure to subjective affect that is *independent of recognition*.'[23]

Another empirical route to the same result was this: the taking of a particular food by an animal is regularly followed by a nausea-inducing agent. The association that this could establish between the taste of the food and nausea was precluded by both administering the nauseating agent and letting it take effect under anaesthesia. Yet even though the animal was never conscious of what followed eating the food, it developed an aversion to the taste of the food.[24] Even if we were to grant that there can be such a thing as an unconscious appraisal of something of which one is (or has been) conscious, it would still be hard to accept that there could be an unconscious appraisal of something of which one never has been made conscious. So there seems little justification for insisting that there must be an appraisal behind the animal's acquired aversion – assuming that the hapless animal's aversion wasn't based rather on the association of the food taste with being subsequently anaesthetised every time!

It is, of course, possible to be aroused by *incomplete* information about the impinging object or circumstance. Fragmentary information (like a sudden report or a rustle) can have meaning (for example, as the signs or ambience of danger).[25] But then one is conscious of and recognises at least the signs or the ambience ('Something is wrong here'). So this capacity to react to the signs before we have fully read them, important though it is, does not preclude the cases in which conscious recognition is altogether absent (the 'don't know why' cases).

At this point the presumption that it is impossible to react to something without being alerted to it and without discriminating at least something about it tempts one to postulate a process of identification and assessment of which the agent is unaware, tantamount to tacit or to unconscious judgement. But in addition to the problem mentioned in the last paragraph, this faces the difficulties noted in the foregoing chapter. We need a reason for superimposing recognition on all reactions: the fact that an (unwitting) act of recognition *would*, if it existed, explain apparently ungrounded emotive arousals does not entail that there *must* be such an act of recognition or that it is what explains them. If we just look for the explanation that would be sufficient, we will find ourselves ascribing to the cyclist the knowledge of what he does to stay upright. Also, there is the problem presented by subjective irrationality: how can a person be supposed to believe furtively what, alerted to the issue, he overtly and confidently rejects?

Recent work in neurophysiology sheds some light on this issue. The study of patterns of fear that are laid down and subsequently rekindled or damped down suggests two layers of causation, each partly independent of the other. The actual fear response in the brain issues from the amygdala. There seem to be two routes by which the amygdala can be excited, one cortical (sensory cortex) and one subcortical (sensory thalamus). The subcortical route involves only a rudimentary perception of the world; it traffics in primitive cues but is thereby more direct and speedy, offering a 'quick and dirty reaction mechanism'.[26] The detour via the cortex provides detailed and accurate representations but is more indirect and is slower. Cortical reaction lags by about one step:

> The thalamus activates the amygdala at about the same time as it activates the cortex. The arrangement may enable emotional responses to begin in the amygdala before we completely recognise what it is we are reacting to or what we are feeling.[27]

Moreover, the neural basis of emotional memory differs from that of 'declarative', that is, conscious, memory. The latter relies on the hippocampus, which may be insufficiently developed in early childhood to permit conscious retrieval of the earliest experiences of fear and the consequent patterning of the person's fear dispositions (which may also be relatively immutable):

> The emotional memory system, which may develop earlier [than the capacity for declarative memory] clearly forms and stores its unconscious memories of these [traumatic] events. And for this reason, the trauma may affect mental and behavioural functions in later life, albeit through processes that remain inaccessible to consciousness.[28]

Notice that,

> Emotional and declarative memories are stored and retrieved in parallel, and their activities are joined seamlessly in our conscious experience. That does not mean that we have direct conscious access to emotional memory; it means instead that we have access to the consequences – such as the way we behave, the way our bodies feel.[29]

This weakens in advance one objection to the evidence for the 'primacy of affect' involving a subject's preferences, namely, that preferences are not emotions. Lazarus alleges that in the research cited by Zajonc the subject's preferences might be a matter of 'intellectual choice' rather than of emotion.[30] While the research may not have taken any steps to provide against this, the possibility of it seems remote. In the first place, the subjects were not asked which tunes they thought *merited* preference. And this would have been a hard question to answer, for the tunes were not lengthy and not heard in the context of complete musical works, so that there were scant grounds on which to form judgements or to do much more than react spontaneously, hot or cold. Nor is there much danger that the animal's acquired taste aversion was really an 'intellectual choice'.

Nevertheless, preferences of this kind are only distant cousins of emotions such as admiration or guilt. Preferences are related to emotions in as much as preferences can involve affect. Certainly they are a restricted sample of emotion, though they are within hailing distance of delectation and disgust. However, the empirical work on preferences that Zajonc cites remains suggestive for emotion more generally if it succeeds in showing that affective responses need not be only to what an experience is understood to mean.

And this possibility shows itself in less tenuous or marginal examples. One of these is controversial but probably shouldn't be. A seemingly simple illustration of the 'primacy of affect' is startle. It occurs almost instantaneously without needing identification of its source or any conclusion as to the nature or extent of threat. (It might be contrasted with astonishment, which does have a clear cognitive structure in the shape of a background of assumptions against which the astonishing thing is seen as hardly possible.) Lazarus proposes to disqualify startle as an emotion by classifying it as a reflex, like knee-jerk or blinking. This is because 'it does not behave like other reactions we call emotions.'[31] Even if this were true, all it proves is that startle differs from other emotions in some respects.[32] As an argument against startle being an emotion, it clearly begs the question. Startle might be an emotional reaction with its own distinctive characteristics. And why should it not? It should be perfectly clear just from the preceding discussion that there is in fact no single way or set of ways in which the other reactions we call emotions behave. Since there are many formal contrasts amongst emotive reactions, a great portion of them would turn out not to be emotions because they didn't behave like the others. (And vice versa for the others, so that there would turn out to be hardly any emotions!) Moreover, for what it is worth, startle actually is one of the reactions we call emotional: 'You gave me a start' is synonymous with 'You gave me a fright', which means just what it says, since the apology, 'Sorry, I didn't mean to frighten you', is apt precisely because an unpleasant spasm of emotion (fright) and temporary distress has been caused. By contrast, reflexes such as knee-jerks and blinks are not notable as emotive experiences. So ordinary usage here, which equates start with fright (an emotion), is no mere semantic accident. However, startle certainly is a reflex; so the correct conclusion should be that some emotions can occur as reflex-like responses.

Apart from its illustrative value, however, startle is only a minor emotive phenomenon. Euphoria and depression are not minor, however. And recent clinical studies confirm that the onset of these emotions can become independent of any cognitive cues. People subject to 'rapid cycling' of these emotional states may experience shifts in them from one extreme to another in days or hours, shifts that come 'out of the blue' or even at fixed intervals.[33] The findings of R. M. Post and others are that 60 per cent of first episodes of depression or mania are indeed preceded by a disturbing event, apprehended as such, giving recognisable ground for depression (though, note, not for mania – it's a sad world); but for second episodes only 30 per cent, decreasing to rapid cycling, where only 6 per cent are reactions to stressful occurrences.[34] As Kramer puts it, 'There are people in whom mood seems to have lost its attachment to any psychological stimulus whatsoever, in whom affect has become utterly dissociated from their experience of the everyday world.'[35]

Once again, it should not be supposed that only people in a disrupted condition respond 'unthinkingly' with emotion. Ordinary fear flickers through ordinary lives. It is familiar and potent and appears to start early, prior to the acquisition of language or the accumulation and comprehension of experience.[36] Starting in the first year, children are progressively susceptible to a variety of directly fear-inducing cues, including abandonment, looming objects, dark passages, sudden unfamiliar noises, darkness, heights, strangers.[37] Clearly, these situations and appearances are loosely associated with the risk of danger, especially in the settings that dominated human evolution. They are actuarially loaded. Equally clearly, they are not known to be such by the frightened child. Even if the child had to perform a cognitive act of sorts to recognise the cue that signals possible peril, this is unlikely to include recognising that danger may lurk, the judgement that would ground the fear. For the children do not yet comprehend what the actual dangers are or even that they exist. Thus, Bowlby records that fear of the dark and of strangers and unfamiliar or abrupt noises and other events becomes pronounced as early childhood progresses, yet the fear specifically of damage or death is almost absent even as late as 12 years of age.[38] Looming, strangeness, darkness and so on, must be able to frighten autonomously, that is, without being construed as portents of danger. (These responses resemble revulsion at tastes and odours from certain foods and other matter that steers us clear of infection and poisoning.) The likelihood of danger would figure in the causal history of the susceptibility to the fears but not in the description of what is frightening the child. What it is frightened of is no different from what frightens it, namely, just the looming, strangeness and so on.

As the parallel with disgust suggests, fear responses to natural cues – 'preferences without inferences' – is not confined to childhood:

> not only through childhood but throughout adolescence and adult life as well the natural clues *and their derivatives* remain among the most effective of all the stimulus situations that arouse fear.[39]

> Most clearly apparent during childhood and old age, sometimes discounted during adult life, these biases nevertheless remain with us. From the cradle to the grave they are an intrinsic part of human nature.[40]

In many personal encounters, first impressions offer common if often unnoticed cases of non-rationalised preference. These are at least as compelling as the experimental studies that favour the 'primacy of affect'. So on this let Zajonc have the last word: 'The remarkable aspect of first impressions of persons is their immediacy. When we meet a stranger, we know within a fraction of a second whether we like the person or not. The reaction is instantaneous and automatic.'[41] The response, though perhaps vague, may be sharp, and it can be swifter than the capacity to locate reasons for it.[42] It may even direct the reflective search for reasons. Nor is the spontaneity of preferences restricted to instant reactions: 'People do not get married or divorced, commit murder or suicide, or lay down their lives for freedom upon a detailed cognitive analysis of the pros and cons of their actions.'[43]

The feat of recognition that figures in our arousal is often all-governing, but it can also be very modest. And it does not tell us what emotive arousal is.

– Notes –

1. Taylor (1975) p. 393 and Lyons (1980), pp. 142–3, not to mention Freud (see Sachs (1974)), settle for this commonsensical way of conceiving of irrational emotion.
2. Milton Clarke, 'Epidemic of Death', *The Arizona Star*, 29 December 1993.
3. Marks (1969), pp. 6 and 232 respectively. See also Farrell (1981).
4. Or still more, to perceive it as danger.
5. Polanyi (1973), pp. 49–50.
6. And discovering that I am committed to something does not seem the same as discovering that I believed it, since realising what a given belief commits me to might be a reason for *withdrawing* that belief, since it has a consequence I would not accept (and therefore, do not accept and have not accepted).
7. See Lycan (1986) and Crimmins (1992), p. 247.
8. That someone should pervasively and consistently fear things or find things disgusting which he saw no grounds to fear or abhor would call into question his sanity, but that does not make this impossible.
9. Crimmins (1992).
10. Wittgenstein (1967), p. 237. Wittgenstein is surely right to complain that 'it is just crazy to think that there is an error here and she believes she has given birth to a child'.
11. Sachs (1974), pp. 143–4.
12. Ibid., p.143. Notice that the claim here is only that thoughts can be unconscious causes or reverberate unconsciously, not that they are the only vehicle for unconscious causation.
13. See Leighton (1985), p. 130. (Also for his discussion of the possibility that the person is simply reacting to conditioning.)
14. Perhaps while *retaining* this idea within the terms of the narrative, a philosophical double-standard that ought to give pause.
15. The term 'construal' for this was suggested by Robert Roberts (1988), pp. 190–1. See also Hampshire (1965), p. 98, 'The man who is frightened of the dark may not believe

that he is in danger: perhaps he knows that he is not; but at the same time he finds that the thought or idea of danger stays in his mind, and that he cannot rid himself of it'; Greenspan (1988), pp. 5–6; and Armon-Jones (1991), ch. 1.

16. Here I am disagreeing with Mounce (1978) who claims that to alarm a person, the loss of his or her wedding ring must occasion the thought that the loss will imperil the marriage. This requirement seems too strong. Being strangely upset by losing the ring seems distinct from thenceforth having a premonition about the marriage or seeing it as blighted by the loss.

17. Perhaps I could envy the person I might have been. However, even this exotic but possible contortion misses the target, for it is not me but only a possible me, an imaginary me that I envy.

18. Lawrence (1986), p. 205.

19. Lazarus (1982), p. 1021.

20. W. Wundt, quoted by Zajonc (1980), p. 152.

21. Work cited by Zajonc (1980), p. 155.

22. Lazarus (1984), p. 124.

23. Zajonc (1980), p. 162, and pp. 162–3 for Zajonc's summary of Wilson's experiment and a follow-up.

24. This experiment, by Garcia and Rusiniak, is cited on p. 120 of Zajonc (1984).

25. But *need* it? For a frog to take fright and spring away, need the sudden ripple nearby have alerted the frog to danger, any more than it informs him that he is the intended prey of a snake, who isn't just passing by. Lazarus speaks here of 'cognitive schemata that signify danger instantly at the sound of a slight rustle in the glass [his example is of a rabbit] or the sight of a dimly perceived shape' (1982), p. 1022. But why can't the sight or sound just galvanise him directly without having to inform him in order to galvanise him? (I am assuming that rabbits and even frogs do not lead affectively denuded lives and are subject to fear; but if that is too rash, the same issue could be raised about higher animals.) If the simpler account is true of frogs, could it never apply to us?

26. LeDoux (1994), p. 56.

27. Ibid., p. 56

28. Ibid., p. 57. It would seem to follow that the phrase 'emotional memory' when applied to the non-cortical formation is something of a misnomer – at best a stretched and dangerously ambiguous usage – since it covers something we are precisely unable to remember! A misnomer especially in light of LeDoux's description of memory as 'the process by which we bring back to mind some earlier conscious experience' (p. 56).

29. Ibid., p. 57.

30. Lazarus (1984), p. 125.

31. Lazarus (1984), p. 124.

32. Being non-judgemental is not among the features that purportedly distinguish startle from (other) emotions. The features identified by Ekman's research are (1) that gunshot consistently elicited startle, whilst there is no single elicitor that unfailingly calls forth any given emotion. The idea seems to be that the source of startle is stereotypical, like knee-jerk, but the source of emotions (rapture, melancholy, etc.) is not. There is everything wrong with this: (a) that x always produces reaction R does not entail that only x ever (or always) produces reaction R. People have startled me in lots of ways without opening fire. (b) Perhaps this generalisation held for Ekman's experimental trials, but *always*? – What about seasoned combat troops? (Here, the problem of induction comes home to roost.) (c) There may be single unfailing elicitors of many emotions, too. Try heaving just about anyone out of an aeroplane without a parachute. For anyone, including even Job, try plucking away and destroying the things prized above all others. Do we have much trouble forecasting the emotions

in these cases (which are, fortunately, beyond the scope of experimental psychology)?

Ekman's other result (2) was that the startle response could not be totally inhibited whereas emotions can. (a) This person presumes that susceptibility to total inhibition is a necessary condition to a response being emotional. What possible ground is there for this requirement (there is, for instance, no basis for it in the *Oxford English Dictionary* entry for 'emotion') than artitrary semantic stipulation? (b) A fortiori, it presumes that *all* emotions can be totally inhibited. Is there exhaustive experimental evidence for this? (Notice that to test it would require delimiting what counts as an emotion, which is what is at issue here.) I propose the same falsifying tests as in the discussion of (1) above: Can a normal person dumped out of an aeroplane without a parachute totally free himself of fear? Can anyone free themselves totally from jealousy when their best beloved's affections become passionately engaged elsewhere? Lazarus' response to this research is this: 'Thus, from the perspective of a relational and cognitive conception of emotion, I think we should exclude startle from the rubric of emotion' (1984), p. 125. The question-begging and semantic legislation are evident. Here, unfortunately, one is forced to recall Wittgenstein's otherwise patronising and often unfair dictum: 'In psychology there are experimental methods and *conceptual confusion*' (1953, II, xiv).

33. Kramer (1993), p. 109.
34. Cited ibid., p. 93.
35. Ibid., p. 108.
36. Bowlby (1973).
37. Ibid.
38. Ibid., p. 117.
39. Ibid., p. 152 (italics mine).
40. Ibid., p. 139.
41. Zajonc (1980), p. 157.
42. Ibid., p. 172.
43. Ibid., p. 172.

CHAPTER 3

Force and Vivacity

What is passionate in us rises and falls, leaps or creeps, and slowly paces. Now it becomes urgent, now hesitant, now stirred more feebly, now more strongly.

Johann Gottfried Herder

– EMOTIONS: COURSE VS CONTENT –

We saw that what a person thinks need not settle what his emotion will be. This potential discrepancy is qualitative. Yet, even when someone's emotions do harmonise in kind with his thoughts, his emotions may still have features the thoughts lack. It is not always possible to extract the characterisation of emotion wholly from the content of the judgements or other thoughts that serve to classify it. Here, the discrepancy is quantitative. There is a dimension of quantity as well as of quality to emotions. Emotions come in degrees of force. The intensity of a given episode of emotion is conspicuously prone to wax and wane. Fear can grow from unease to anxiousness and rise through fright, dread, terror to panic; anger can swell from irritation to vexation, and through aggravation, rage and fury to frenzy.

The level of an emotion's intensity and the changes in this needn't be reflected in the person's thoughts. For, these differences in degree are not always a precise function of the kind of appraisals one accepts at the time. An emotional reaction can overdo or underplay what the person's actual views strictly warrant and be either faint-hearted or overblown. A person can be angry without being as angry as he might or even should be under the circumstances (which include his beliefs). Someone who says he is 'rather cross' at something grossly affronting ('Actually, I suppose it *is* rather outrageous, when you think of it') needn't be dissembling or understating his actual emotion. And if he is not, this isn't necessarily because he views the offending event in some attenuated way which others who think he is underreacting don't appreciate; for he may wonder at himself that he isn't downright furious ('I really ought to be furious' is perfectly intelligible). Conversely, an emotion may oversell rather than underfill its cognitive frame: fury where annoyance belongs ('flying off the handle'). One may try to get a grip on oneself precisely because one grasps the disproportion of one's reaction. Finally, one's emotion can alter, veering from overreaction or underreaction to a reaction more in keeping with the perceived gravity of the situation, or from that to either excess, without variation in one's thought, as self-addressed injunctions to achieve perspective often attest ('Cool down!'/'What's *wrong* with me?!'). And where changes in the acuteness of an emotion do accommodate to changes of mind, they may do so only lingeringly. My palpitations may subside in the wake of a mollifying explanation rather than with it. The magnitude and volatility of an emotion can set it apart.

There can be upwellings of force in an emotion even where there are no relevant thoughts at all: 'She reported an increase in her sense of undirected urgency. Overcome with cravings, she did not know what she craved. She had to do something, yet she did not know what.'[1] Need there *be* anything she longed for, or ground for her longing, if (as here) she could be stirred to these promptings by medication? When they are forceful, inarticulate stirrings may grasp at straws. Sometimes, an emotionally aroused person's *perception* of their situation is *post hoc*: People often seek to *confer* intelligibility and direction on their emotions, casting about for interpretations and outlets or trying to fabricate them. This – one of the hazards of psychotherapy – can be a source of much futility.[2]

– THOUGHTS: FIERCE AND FAINT –

Some philosophers argue that the liveliness of an emotion can still be a feature of its attendant thoughts even if it isn't a feature of their propositional content.[3] This is clearly unpromising for the 'blind' reactions just mentioned, but what about the larger class? Thus, Solomon, who has defended the centrality of *judgements* to emotions recognises that emotions aren't just any judgements but 'intense' judgements.[4] This would make unintense emotions hard to accommodate. But what about the others? How does one 'passionately' believe something, believe with 'all one's heart'? (Note that 'passionate' believings are typically believings *in* rather than believings *that*.) What could be meant by an 'intense judgement' other than a judgement that attributes much importance to something (which the scale of one's emotional reaction, again, can fail to fit)? When 'fervently' in 'fervently believes' is not a way of attaching importance to what is believed, it indicates either that the believer has no doubts about what he believes or that holding the belief is important (for example, belief in God). But this isn't the same as being emotional (or even having emotion). Emotion, and its fervour, arises in consequence of this kind of conviction.

This is not the only way of trying to capture the energy of emotion in cognitive terms, however. The degree of an emotion could still be presented in terms of *how* one thinks of something rather than *what* one thinks of it. The thought of something (such as your conduct at the party) can be highly focused or vague; meticulously attentive and vivid or less so. Accordingly, disproportion between one's thoughts and the magnitude of one's emotion might be sought in a disproportion between the degree of attention one bestows on the object of the thoughts and the degree of attention it actually deserves given one's view of it. 'I concentrate my thoughts of the object to an extent that is not warranted by the situation' or 'my degree of concentration falls short of what is warranted'.[5] Undoubtedly, lingering upon or passing over what one knows about the object of an emotion can result in a change, a heightening or an ebbing. And this can be an important device for emotional self-control. Hatred is nourished by allowing the occasioning offence to prey on one's mind (or by fastening one's mind on it).

In such cases, however, the degree of concentration is not the degree of the emotion but the cause of the degree of the emotion. After all, due (or even undue) attention may *fail* to ensure a reaction of appropriate degree. Also it may well be true that someone in the grip of an excessive emotion is excessively preoccupied with – 'makes too much of' – the object or some undeserving feature of it, but far from constituting the force of the emotion, the undue fixation may instead be produced and explained by that force. (Why am I obsessed by his remark/by that image? – Because of how much it disturbed me.) The relation can even be one of feedback: the passion of the zealot at once dictates the focus of his attention and gets rationalised and fortified as a result of that. Impassioned, one may choose to dwell on what best sustains the passion. And this fact, that emotion can actually motivate the deployment of attention, is what can make *due* concentration a grudging concession, difficult to achieve or sustain.

Is there no way, then, in which the waxing and waning of an emotion could be shown to consist in changes in the person's judgements? In particular, could episodic shifts in the received force of an emotion mark changes in judgement that do not just come down to replacing one judgement with another? In her discussion of the Stoic approach to the emotions in her book *The Therapy of Desire*, Martha Nussbaum suggests how this might be. To be an emotion, according to Nussbaum (citing Chrysippus), a judgement must be as yet unspoiled, undigested – it must be 'fresh'.[6] For a judgement to be 'fresh', Nussbaum suggests, is for it to be still unintegrated, not yet accommodated by the rest of what the person accepts. Emotion is a crisis of intellectual structure, each emotion being a homeless newcomer to a community of established thought. Appraisals we are unprepared for, those which occur starkly, are what we register as emotions. My acceptance that a loved one has died and that this loss is grievous becomes grief when it confronts the settled and lingering expectations that I will see this person again, that the life that includes him will go on as before, and so on. And the grief wanes as these habitual suppositions are relinquished and the new realities are acknowledged. Once the rest of what I think accommodates to the judgement that I have lost and lost heavily, my mind ceases to be 'assaulted' by it; the judgement moves from grief to become, presumably, resignation.

Increments in emotional intensity might also arise from changes in the beliefs that surround a particular judgement: my realisation that I have been left off your guest list moves from shoulder-shrugging emotive neutrality to disappointment when I learn of all the desirable people who were invited; and the acuteness of the disappointment will depend on just *how* long and select the list is.

If the idea that an emotion is a cognitively anomalous judgement were itself plausible, it could account for changes in the level of an emotion in a person who continues to judge in the same way. (My grief can diminish – or vary – without my changing my mind about the loss.) As the surrounding beliefs shifted, the degree of anomalousness of the same judgement, and with that its emotive punch, could shift. However, this whole picture of emotions as disrupted relations amongst beliefs inverts what actually happens. The fact that a beloved person has died can be assented to without yet being 'taken in'. 'Taking in' the fact does indeed involve realising and accepting its implications – that the certainties of the relationship are gone, that the things so cherished are lost. And these realisations are a matter of degree. They can be more or less extensive. But the bare ('fresh'), *un*-'taken in', realisation of loss *may* be emotively numb at first; whilst the effect of 'taking in' the new realisation *will* be just the opposite of calming – as the extent of the loss dawns, grief deepens (the same goes for fear, anger or jealousy, for instance). It is with the death of all the old cherished expectations as well as of the person that the grief reaches its fullest force.

It seems that the attempt to cast emotions as assentings (judgements or beliefs) fails to capture their susceptibility to degrees of intensity (or the volatility of these swings). Yet this is surely at least as pervasive and striking a feature of emotions as their representational character. But there is more to thought than assent and propositional content assented to. It is possible to see or characterise something in terms that one would not actually accept as true of it. These imaginings and appearances can be emotively evocative and evocative to greater or lesser degrees (depending on the images and descriptions, their vivacity, luridness and the like). Here, the style of the thought matters as much as its content. We noticed in the last chapter that such thoughts, which Robert Roberts calls 'construals', don't account for qualitative discrepancies between emotions and judgements. We must now ask whether the degrees of emotion, with which they certainly resonate, indeed reside in them?

That appearances, imaginings, pictures and constructions put on things can be emotive does not mean they are emotions. How may we understand reports like this: 'I can't bear it (that is, my remorse and distress) when I think of the look of shock in those deep, sensitive eyes and the pained disbelief in his face when I let him down.' It does not seem right to identify my remorse with my image of him at the moment of betrayal; it is more a trigger. Even if we said that the pain inscribed in the image of his stricken face is at once the pain of his realisation and that of my remorse, the possibility remains that what the image does is to *express* the pain of the situation for each of us. But it is unclear that my remorse, which *is* expressed (as well as revived or intensified) by how I remember the event also consists in this.

The psychological trait of oversensitivity sheds some light on this question as to how separable an emotion is from the thoughts laden with it and where the locus of its intensity lies. The acuteness with which emotion is experienced may account for the trait of oversensitivity in certain of its forms. Hypersensitivity to personal rejection by others (and hence morbid fear of it) invites both cognitive and non-cognitive explanations. Thus, the person for whom the menace of personal rejection looms relentlessly and unreasonably may just have a sharper eye than most for minor and subtle signs of it given out, wittingly or unwittingly, by others (the cognitive explanation). On the other hand (the non-cognitive explanation), his sensitivity might reflect the sharpness of the anguish induced by rejection and promised by the slightest sign of it. This latter possibility has the advantage of *explaining* the person's 'overdeveloped' power to discern (or construe) ominous cues. This view of the matter is reinforced by the success in reducing the fear of rejection by pharmacologically blunting the person's vulnerability to pain. It is found that once the person is no longer so hard *hit* by rejection or the thought of it, *perceptions* of it cease to crowd the person's mind. The core of the fear is not the kind of thoughts he has but the severity of the impact these have on him, which can vary independently. The internal amplifier controls the external receiver.[7]

The conclusion must be that the magnitude or acuteness of emotion need not be reflected in what the person actually thinks. And so, it cannot *be* that.

– EMOTIVE FORCE AS DESIRE –

Could the energic aspect of emotion be *desire*, already identified as an extra-cognitive candidate in Chapter 1? Desires, like emotions, can be tepid or fierce. And they are similarly volatile. At any rate, a desire needn't accord with better judgement, and it can veer in force, leaving better judgement standing. Again, shifts in the degree of an emotion are shifts in its motivational force. Might that not come down to shifts in the keenness of desire? At least in paradigmatic cases, emotions might be just those judgements (or other formations of thought) which are imbued by desire: 'How delectable!'/'Get that away from me!'

We might try to refine the view of emotions as 'intense' judgements by using desire to mark off a class of non-dispassionate judgements, which are coextensive with emotions.[8] Perhaps emotions (at least as types) do have representings at their core but not by way of detached contemplation. To amount to emotion, the cognitions have to be completed by desire – desire is the key to attachment.[9] Thinking you have betrayed me is not enough to make me angry with you; *wanting* your loyalty is what transforms your betrayal from a cool fact to a bitter blow.

A footing in desire does offer to explain many of the formal differences between emotions and thoughts (the latter can be dispassionate even as value-judgements and disinterested even as fantasies). Desires can conflict with one another and show stubborn immunity to the influence of reflection. Desires, and with them emotions (but not detached thoughts), have degrees of intensity and can persist even when irrational.[10]

Can desire succeed here where thought on its own fails? That the relations between desire and emotion are close is obvious; what these relations are is less so. Indeed, certain generic differences suggest themselves: there seems a contrast at the level of intentionality. Some emotional states can subsist in recognisable form without being directed at objects, as in moods (mellowness, lightness of heart, tension, melancholy); but it is less clear that one could similarly be prey to a desire that wasn't for anything. Also, the behaviour, if any, to which I am directly impelled in a given state of emotion serves to express the emotion, not to satisfy it; whereas what I want as host to a given desire serves rather to satisfy the desire than to express it (*satisfaction* and *expression* are not interchangeable here).

What then are their relations? A minimal claim would be that having certain desires is a condition of having certain emotions.[11] Hope is a representative example. For instance, some emotions seem *explained* by particular types of desire – disappointment and/or bitterness arise from thwarted desire. Here, at least, desires need a priority and logical independence in relation to the emotion. On the other hand, some desires need explaining, and this can require reference to the person's emotional state, where that state is not to be understood in turn by allusion to yet another desire or set of desires. The condition of depression offers a complex but important case in point.

– DESIRE, DEPRESSION AND THE MAGNITUDE OF EMOTION –

Suppose an individual is set on killing himself, but for no reason that others can understand; his actual setbacks and problems seem too trivial to warrant so drastic a step. The explanation is that he is undergoing major depression. This could be seen as itself dissolving into an explanation in terms of desires. For, what is germane here about depression is the weight of despair: he wants to escape his despair by the only means that offers itself. And despair might be represented as generalised negative desire, that is, desiring nothing anywhere (or desiring only disengagement from everything attention lights upon). In fact, it might be seen as consisting in a desire for release from this condition of pervasive desirelessness.

Perhaps, yet this is not quite the tale a depressive may live to tell. In the condition of acute depression, the elements that typically make for emotion are magnified. If we focus on the emotional aspect of this condition, the role of desire is indeed prominent. The depressed mind seems to find the world stripped of all charm, offering nothing. This desireless state in which nothing is worth wanting is anything but a state of wanting for nothing, of a release in Nirvana. It is intolerable; it is a state in which its victim acutely desires not to be.

Now while the longing to escape the merciless bleakness of this landscape of undesire captures some of the hopelessness of depression, it does not capture all of it. As William Styron depicts it in *Darkness Visible*, the world the depressed person craves to escape is not just dead but dismal, and actively so, in a peculiarly elusive and excruciating way.[12] The intensity of the desire just reflects the degree of the felt anguish.

An account of the anatomy of depression in terms of desires is not self-sufficient. The pivotal feature of this state is how it *feels*.

> I was feeling in my mind a sensation close to, but indescribably different from, actual pain.[13]

> What I had begun to discover is that, mysteriously and in ways that are totally remote from normal experience, the grey drizzle of horror induced by depression takes on the quality of physical pain. But it is not an immediately identifiable pain, like that of a broken limb.[14]

And this can achieve an apotheosis of quality and intensity: 'sitting in the living room, I experienced a curious inner convulsion that I can only describe as despair beyond despair. It came out of the cold night; I did not think such anguish possible.'[15]

It is true that certain thoughts are also present. There is a value-judgement – objectively irrational – as to personal worthlessness ('The loss of self-esteem is a celebrated symptom'[16]) and calamity at every hand ('a state of unrealistic hopelessness, torn by exaggerated ills and fatal threats that bear no resemblance to actuality'[17]). And there is a represen-tation of the misery itself as intractable. Styron actually records this thought, that relief is unobtainable, as the source of the impulse to suicide. The judgement that available outside help does not help might well predispose someone to this view – Styron's own final descent followed a particularly futile psychiatric consultation.[18]

However, while the downward path may pass trough a characteristic landscape of thought that issues in a craving for oblivion, this may not explain the journey. Here, in Peter Kramer's account, is what happened when an anti-depressant was prescribed to a man whom psychotherapy had failed to relieve of increasing feelings of 'groundless free-floating anxiety' and low self-esteem:

> The patient's low self-esteem, which had been present since his earliest child-hood, began to disappear. He began to re-evaluate his aptitudes and assents in a thoroughly realistic manner. The insights gained in psychotherapy, which heretofore had no emotional impact, were now accompanied by a different attitude toward himself. It was as if William M. had been subtly depressed

throughout his life and as if his low self-esteem had been a superficial manifestation of the depression.[19]

Kramer observes that,

> For William M., psychotherapy was useful only when he was on medication; off antidepressants, he was unable to use insight. The beliefs that accompany low self-esteem – I am a failure, what I have achieved is of no importance – appeared and disappeared, or gained and lost potency, in conjunction with the changed feeling regarding the self.[20]

And note, here the feeling was a pharmacological rather than a cognitive effect.

As for the victim's perception of his plight (namely, that it is hopeless and thus unendurable), he needn't even purport to found that on evidence. This apprehension (perhaps as a construal) is forged more directly out of properties of the dysphoria itself. It is unrelenting, undeflectable and all-encompassing:

> despair, owing to some evil trick played upon the sick brain by the inhabiting psyche, comes to resemble the diabolical discomfort of being imprisoned in a fiercely overheated room. And because no breeze stirs this caldron, because there is no escape from this smothering confinement, it is entirely natural that the victim begins to think ceaselessly of oblivion.[21]

Note that it is these qualities themselves, as distinct from just a recognition that the dysphoria possesses them, that induces the hopelessness.

In sum, the depressed person's belief that his condition is hopeless, his appraisal of it as intolerable (the 'despair beyond despair') and his desire for oblivion are accountable to what he *feels* and the way this feeling comes at him. Desire here arises from the experience of intolerable distress that has to be escaped at all costs. It is not, for instance, a desire to escape from the fact of desirelessness but to escape pain.

The potential explanatory precedence of emotion over desire is not confined to the example of clinical depression. A simpler and less harrowing example would be adoring a child. One does not come to adore a particular child by first wanting to behold, caress and cherish it. One wants to do these things as a result of having been charmed and thereby brought to adore.

Jennifer Robinson replies to this form of criticism of the desires approach to emotions as follows:

The main objection . . . might be that I have got things back to front: it is not desires that determine judgements or conceptions, but judgements or conceptions that determine desires. For example, it would seem that when I am afraid of the approaching grizzly bear, I make a (dispassionate) judgement that it is dangerous, and I have a desire to escape from the danger, which is a *consequence* of that judgement. If I am right, however, even in this commonplace example [sic!], the reverse is true. If I am afraid of the bear, this entails that I have an intense desire to stay alive and unharmed and to avoid threatening situations, and it is these desires and goals that determine the way I think of the bear: I conceive of it as a threat to these deeply held desires. By contrast, if I am excited and exultant when I see the bear, then I have desires to court danger and to test my courage which are more intense than my desire to stay alive and unharmed, and it is these desires and goals which determine how I think of the bear, as an opportunity for me to exercise my wits and my courage. In both cases I conceive of the bear as dangerous, but it is only if I have an intense desire to avoid danger that I am afraid: the conception does not cause the desire but vice versa.[22]

While it is true that if I am afraid of the bear then I have an intense desire to stay alive and uninjured, it isn't obvious that the fear has to be a *consequence* of the desire. In fact there is reason to deny this. For what is to explain which desires are present and which are most intense at the moment of the encounter? One thing that can account for these facts is my emotional state (occurrent or dispositional). Why, for instance, is the desire to avoid the danger and escape the more intense desire (when it is)? Because the immanence of maiming or death – or perhaps more realistically, the mere sight of such a beast rounding on me – scares the daylights out of me.

Reference to my emotional state may also be necessary to explain the balance of my desires, since a given desire may underdetermine a person's emotional state. Thus, why am I seized by the desire to court danger and test my courage? *Either* because I fear less for my life than for my honour *or* because the challenge thrills me – struggling against mortal danger gives me a unique high.[23]

These considerations are not meant to oppose the general thesis that desires cause emotions with a general counter-thesis that emotions cause desires. Too often the desires and the emotions are not separable as causes and effects. Wanting certain things is characteristic of having a given emotion to the point that in some cases wanting them is a condition of the emotion's being of the type that it is (love, hate). Sometimes it seems arbitrary whether a state is called a desire or an emotion: lust is as much a desirous passion as a passionate desire. Perhaps all intense desires should be regarded as emotions, as the words 'longing', 'craving' and 'voracious' suggest. For their part, although desires can be ambiguous as to what emotion they reflect, it would often be scarcely conceivable how someone could be susceptible to certain desires without being subject to a given emotion, for example, how the desire to do every kind of harm to a particular individual could not bespeak hatred. Nor is it that the desires are just effects or signs of the emotion; it does not belong to *hatred* to be free of such desires.

So why not just identify hate with the desire to injure its target (for his perceived or presumed offensiveness)? This would go too far. One could desire to injure it without desiring this out of hate. And other things than desires can amount to hate, for example, obsessive, brooding attention to the odiousness of the person, resistance to balanced judgements of him, hostile fantasies and, not least, a disposition to sentiments of loathing, to accesses of spite – that is, to particular feelings.

– Notes –

1 Kramer (1993), p. 102.

2. A related example is found in Emma Bovary's struggle to give form to her racking discontent:

> She had bought herself a blotting-pad, writing case, pen-holder and envelopes, though she had no one to write to. She dusted the shelves, looked at herself in the glass, picked up a book, then started dreaming between the lines and let it drop in her lap. She longed to travel – or to go back to the convent. She wanted to die, and she wanted to live in Paris.
>
> (Flaubert (1971), p. 73)

3. A related possibility is discussed at length below in Chapter 5.

4. Solomon (1993), p. 187.

5. Taylor (1975), p. 393. The more intense an emotion is, the more its object will tend to absorb our attention, and the more the value we attach to this object will be magnified. And the extent of absorption and the inflation of importance here may exceed what one judges appropriate. Nash has made these facts the basis of a cognitive account of what emotions typically are, an account that purports to avoid the problems of judgement-based cognitive theories. 'What makes some evaluation/desire complex emotional . . . is the presence of a focused attention of a particular sort on the object of the emotion, resulting in the agent's overevaluation of that object (relative to his dispassionate evaluation of it)': Nash (1989), p. 482. The cognitions of a person in a state of intense occurrent emotion may well be like this, but that does not make them constitutive of the emotion they signal. Even if a thing couldn't assume undue proportions for an emotionally quiescent person and always did so for an aroused person, that could reflect primarily causal ties between the cognition and the emotion. That I fear x (an aspect of a situation) is *why* it, and the danger in it, obsesses me. And where my emotional state is not what explains my attentional fixation, it may

be explained by it: fixed on x, which looms large for me, I start to panic (and become the more obsessed with x, in a feedback loop). There is also the question as to what valuations are when they are not judgements and perhaps fail to reflect these. If valuations fail to be judgements precisely by being just emotive, then where this happens it will be unedifying to present the emotion as a non-judgemental valuation. Independent content needs to be given then to what *just being emotive* comes to then. I will contend that this is indeed the form commonly taken by non-judgemental valuations. My argument will be that the notion of emotive feeling, once disentangled from cognition, provides the independent content required.

6. Nussbaum (1993), p. 381.
7. Kramer (1993), pp. 103–4. As Kramer puts it,

> once we turn down the amplification, small slights, even if they are noticed for a moment, may pass without being registered into memory. If they are not remembered, it is as if they never happened. In this sense, a secondary effect of reduced amplification is reduced perception. If the recurrent pain can be muted, a sensitive person ought to become less apprehensive, and perhaps less apprehending as well.

(p. 104)

8. A suggestion developed by Robinson (1983).
9. Ibid., pp. 731, 737.
10. Ibid., pp. 734–6.
11. To be sure, this needs refining. For instance, a condition of a certain emotion may be *having had* a certain desire, where the emotion (such as gloating) constitutes the satisfaction the person takes in a fulfilled desire.
12. Styron (1991), pp. 16–17.
13. Ibid., p. 16.
14. Ibid., p. 50.
15. Ibid., p. 63.
16. Ibid., p. 56.
17. Ibid., p. 76.
18. Ibid., p. 60.
19. Wender and Klein (1981), pp. 46–8. Quoted in Kramer (1993), p. 203.
20. Kramer (1993), p. 203.
21. Ibid., p. 50.
22. Robinson (1983), p. 739.
23. Note that how I think of the bear encounter at the time is also insufficient to determine what my emotion towards it is – insufficient causally and conceptually. I could think of the encounter as a challenge (perhaps heaven – appointed) to show my mettle and still succumb.

CHAPTER 4

Putting the Feeling back into Emotion

– A ROLE FOR FEELING? –

What more can there be to an emotion than the judgements or other thoughts that ground it? This question was raised and possible answers surveyed in Chapter 1. Our investigation into this so far has been heavy with negative lessons. Emotions are indeed distinct from the relevant judgements, from which they can become unmoored. Nor can they be accommodated then as construals that might form a cognitively dissonant subtext to the person's actual beliefs. Neither is the volatile flux of emotion – its dynamics – satisfactorily tracked by the cognitive attitudes at either of these two levels. Nor do these difficulties seem resolvable by viewing emotions as desires.

Yet emotions are directable at objects, and they are somehow valuational (even serenity is no mere state of detached contemplation). How can they be valuings without being judgements of value? And how can they be non-dispassionate valuings unless they are desires? – The approach via desires was at least a gesture at capturing the arousal and quality of urgency that distinguishes emotive appraisal from detached appraisal.

The remaining candidate for the extra-cognitive heart of emotion was feeling. And this, the affective charge characteristic of a given sort of emotion, does seem capable of the two kinds of variance with its attendant thoughts, of which we have seen emotions to be capable. The fear in someone who *sees* nothing to fear (for example, from phobic objects, eerie places or corpses) is *felt* all the same; and fear it undoubtedly is. In the last chapter, we saw that in depression the sheer dysphoria of it can play a primary and distinctive role in relation to both the affected person's thoughts and to his desires.

This is not to identify emotion with feeling or to disregard thought as a formative element in emotions. The question is whether emotive feeling can be assimilated to it or is something independent which must precipitate out of thoughts, perceptions and valuations for actual emotion to precipitate, and is something in which some episodes of emotion largely consist.

How well, then, does the claim that feeling is what is emotive about emotions bear up? Let us review it in relation to those features of emotions that we have found resist being understood in other ways.

– THE REALITY OF EMOTIONAL AFFECT –

It is true that an emotion such as anger can arise and persist in unimpassioned form and even be powerful in that form, its power consisting in its relentlessness and capacity to motivate drastic actions. That is not, however, *all* that can be meant by the power of an emotion. An emotional state *can* be impassioned. The anger that cannot be devoid of aroused feeling is the anger that comes in an upsurge, flash or wave, the anger that *sweeps* a person. When I *rue* what I did, my regret amounts to more than just a contrite view of the matter. Some words for emotions actually single out states of emotional feeling: 'anguish', 'glow of affection', 'leaden gloom', 'furious' (as distinct from 'cross') 'ecstatic', 'sorrow' (which 'being sad that . . .' needn't involve). In experiencing feelings of an emotion, we are 'in a state', for example, touched, moved, struck, excited, stirred, aroused. We can be moved 'in the depths of the heart', as distinct from being (also) moved to conclude something, decide something, or to act. The excitement can be physical (trembling, tension, starts) but it needn't be (wistfulness); and many bodily feelings such as itching or dizziness are not distinctively emotional. But some feelings are, be they bodily or not.[1]

Sometimes, in fact, an emotion cannot be ascribed unless the person is (or is prone to get) impassioned with it. *Feeling* the emotion is a condition of *having* it. I could accept what has happened as a pity, regard it as the worst turn and wish things had been otherwise, yet without being moved or upset by it; I feel nothing. (I am perfectly sincere in these attitudes even if detached.) If I am thus 'sorry' but not sad, I lack sorrow, the emotion.[2]

These observations do not, of course, amount to a definition or theory of emotional feeling. If possible at all, that would be pointless until we are satisfied that the notion cannot be eliminated or recast.

– FEELING AND EMOTIONAL FORCE –

The challenge to cognitive conceptions of emotion set out in the last chapter was that even where the kind of emotion a person has may suit the thoughts he has, its keenness may not. What is it that gets out of proportion? Thoughts may be rushed and they may exaggerate, and emotions can get out of hand in this way. However, quantitative mismatch involves disproportion between the adjudged (or seeming) import of something and the magnitude of the emotional response to it. Obviously, the judgement (or construal) is not out of proportion to itself (whether or not it is reasonable in light of the available grounds for it). What can it be about the emotion, then, which is feeble or overwrought? The natural answer is: the degree of feeling in it. Whatever else we may need to say about feeling, it patently does admit of distinctions and fluctuations of degree and strength. The passion of an emotion is normally a matter of how acutely it is felt.

The acuteness that feeling lends emotion could be confused with the motivational strength of a desire but should not be. The capacity of a given desire to capture one's preferences in the teeth of countervailing desires is certainly a matter of degree and is subject to swings. But unlike aroused feeling, it needn't be palpable. Unconscious and instinctual desires or drives can have (often high) degrees of motivational force and yet manifest themselves only in patterns of behaviour; so may ordinary desires, especially desires attaching to habits. The degree of intensity possessed by feeling does contribute to the motivational force of an emotion, often tellingly; but it is a matter of subjective strength, evoked by such notions as poignancy, piercingness, keenness, rankness, faintness, deadness (in psychiatry, 'flatness of affect').[3]

– FEELING AND VALUATION –

Having feelings about something is valuational in that, almost truistically, it is a way of not being indifferent to it, perhaps the keenest way. When a person responds with feeling, his concern becomes more than mere realisation of what the situation warrants; he is stirred by it. The urgency is palpable, not just perceived. Thus, the wish of one person to matter to another is usually the wish to evoke emotion in them, by which they are moved or touched. Of the marks one can leave this is the deepest.

Could a feeling *be* evaluative, however, without being an appraising thought – a value-judgement, an adulatory or derogating image? Well, it can sit uneasily with these. Precisely because of them, my turn of feeling may strike me as odd or offensive (as in the example of Ursula's reactions to Hermione in the passage from *Women in Love* quoted at the end of Chapter 2). Most importantly, however, a feeling can be evaluative where the concern integral to it is not detachable from being felt. For the concern actually takes the form of having the feeling, of being moved in a particular way (or being disposed to this). Being filled with dread is one way of minding a menace. Being galled is a particular way of minding an offence. Feelings are valuings of the things evoking them in as much as they are sui generis ways these things matter to us (part of a thing's goodness or badness is how it makes us feel, namely thrilled, disgusted, dismal and so on).

So instead of registering the value which the object of the feeling can be deemed to have independently of the feeling, the feeling may, indeed, confer that value on the object in the sense that part of the value the object has is precisely dependent on the feeling it commands. The loveliness or charm of a thing enchants us; but these qualities of it are themselves inseparable from this spell they work on us. We do not always feel as we do about a thing because of how it matters when considered independently of what it makes us feel. Where this is so, feelings might be termed constructive valuations. This is why 'understanding' the way certain things matter, the value in them (the true horror of x, the peculiar charm of y), requires having the requisite feelings.

Of course, what the object is (or is seen as being) independently may cause the feeling, but it can do this without constituting or entering into what is felt about the object – without being the quality the object is felt as having. Consider some of the qualities things seem to disclose to us through our feelings towards them: uncanny, scary, disgusting, freaky, adorable, sweet. One could try to list properties that things have to have in order to have these felt qualities, though not with equal hope of success in each case. The *scary* must seem menacing; the *uncanny* and the *disgusting* are harder, but perhaps involve, respectively, danger present but unfathomable and undisclosed, and the intrusion of the impure into the pure; the *freaky* must be peculiar and, well, unsettling; the *sweet* and the *adorable* are especially elusive, and perhaps the best we can do is to name necessary conditions such as ingenuousness and vulnerability. Even if successful, however, the knowledge this project would yield need not of itself enable a person (still less an interplanetary anthropologist) actually to find things uncanny and so on. *Scary* is the way a menace seems to one whom it alarms. *Disgusted* is what it is like to find disgust-evoking qualities disgusting. They are not disgusting except as they disgust. More one cannot say. Indeed, for some feelings the perceptual model of an object and a quality of it detected via a sensitive capacity scarcely suggests itself. Slime may seem disgusting or a fault contemptible, but it is I who am full of spite, the target of my spite isn't. And no exciting object has the kick or thrill it gives (even when the exciting object happens to be someone else's kick or thrill).

This allows us to see how it is that emotions can bypass or flout the thoughts that would rationalise them (see Chapter 2). Because a feeling is a state of a person, rather than a representation of some independent property of an object, it does not have the same kind of fit to the aspects of the world which arouse it that a thought has to the aspect of the world it is about. How one feels may or may not serve to present a state of affairs outside itself; my unease, joy or gloom may but needn't be a reflection on the world beyond (in this, feelings do compare to sensations such as pains, nausea and bitterness). Since a feeling does not just represent, it need not purport to fit. This is why it need not depend on the beliefs that are held. Feelings are causally related to what arouses them, and cognition is one, but only one, of the causal elicitors. Hence the notorious liability of feelings (and hence emotions involving them) to 'blindness'. A rage, a giddy thrill, a trough of depression, a jolt of lust can numb the mind to rational dissuasion. Blindness is possible because feeling is responsive to a range of causes which are peripheral to one's thoughts, yet which may enjoy inordinate evocative powers. These include such psychological byways as association, symbolism and even chemistry.[4]

Emotional feelings, then, can mark values by conferring (creating) them rather than by recognising them, and they can have a wayward causation. But if this is how emotions *can* fail to be a function of the cognitions appropriate to them, why *do* they ever do this? Part of the answer is that feelings themselves have value. Because of what they are variously like to those host to them, they are themselves desirable and undesirable in a host of ways, some of which are themselves matters of feeling. Thus, feeling filled by hate or fear can make one feel disturbed or depressed; indignation can be thrilling; disgust distresses. At a second-order level, one feeling can stand to another as they all stand to their usual objects and hence matter to the one who has them in the same way they make the world matter to him. I can feel frightened of my anger or even get angry at my loss of temper. I can be thrilled by fear (and watch horror films) or be distressed by it (and shun such films).

Errol Bedford pointed out that emotion words are part of our vocabulary of appraisal and criticism.[5] It needs to be added that, in some cases, the valuations emotions embody may be conveyed only by those parts of our critical vocabulary that are expressive of feeling.

– FEELING AND INTENTIONALITY –

The allusions above to objects of feeling on the one hand, and to the non-representational status of feelings on the other, prompt the question whether emotional feelings are intentional (as sensations, for example, are not)? It seems clear that *emotions* typically are: their usual complement of thoughts ensures that they are directed at and about something. Yet it is precisely when emotions are shorn of their governing thoughts, or are out of proportion to them, that they most clearly involve feeling, to the point of consisting of sheer feeling (for example, the 'mindless' panic that spreads through the mob). What, then, of the feelings: are they (like sensations) divorced from all thought and without reference to anything outside themselves?

The answer is that feelings are intentional, but incompletely so. Feelings are capable of precipitating as if from nowhere ('out of the blue'), certainly not by anything the person thinks; and they are capable of not being about anything. The fact that this is puzzling when it happens ('Why should I be in this state?') shows that it is anomalous, however. States of feeling can be and usually are directed at objects, particular or general, real or imaginary. Normally, I am shocked, hurt, excited, anxious *at* or *about* what I am shocked, and so on, *by*. A feeling can be not only a reaction to how things are perceived (as can an accelerated pulse rate), it can also be a way of taking account of this (as an acceleration in pulse rate isn't). In fact, the terms in which things are apprehended seems integral to at least many feelings; feeling shocked, aghast or relieved, for instance, all presuppose a background of expectations and values.

So far, so good. Emotional feelings can have directedness (at the unexpected, horrifying or desired). They can, however, have a peculiar relationship to the thoughts they bear. In writing about emotion, Anthony Kenny declares,

> I have been purporting to give an account of the way in which the concept of an emotion was linked with non-emotional concepts. But in describing the props on which the concept of 'fear' stood I used expressions such as 'fearful circumstances', 'symptoms of fear' so that it may have looked as if my account was circular. I used such expressions merely for brevity; they could be replaced,

without loss of explanatory force, by expressions which make no mention of fear. 'Fearful circumstances', for instance, could be replaced by 'dangerous circumstances'; the concept of *danger* does not involve reference to the emotions . . .'[6]

In the preceding section we saw that in the case of *feelings* this is just what cannot be relied on. Often, what elicits a feeling cannot be adequately characterised except as a thing which invites *that* feeling ('It's just, well, off-putting, yucky'). Here, what one feels towards something is an essential ingredient of how one apprehends it. Two kinds of feeling, for instance, might not be distinguishable by differences in the thoughts distinctive of them (as the emotions of shame and embarrassment are); not, that is, independently of contrasts in what these feelings are like, their experiential content. One person finds snakes, even harmless ones, quietly horrifying, whilst another is disgusted by them. Their aversive feelings are rather different, the first person being 'chilled' but not 'nauseated', the second person vice versa. (Neither need have an independent reason for either the basic aversion or for his version of it.) So where feelings are constructive valuations, the specification of the feeling's intentionality collapses into a specification of its content; its identity will turn on this.

How we should conceive of feelings in light of all these considerations will be the topic of the next three chapters. The first possibility is the most tempting to many. It is that states of feeling themselves must still be seen as thoughts of a special kind.

– NOTES –

1. To speak of what a person may feel in having a particular emotion (or of 'feeling the emotion of grief' or of 'having' feelings) is not to invoke a perceptual use of 'to feel' (as in feeling for my watch, feeling to silk or a weight on my shoulders) – something Ryle warned against (Ryle, 1951). In the perceptual use, what is felt is something independent of my feeling it. With emotional feelings there is no such distinction: what I feel (sorrowful, for instance) and my feeling it are the same. Also, it is true that sometimes what we say we feel (for example, at ease, or better) is actually the absence or cessation of other feelings (ibid., p. 195). Obviously, however, for this to be true sometimes, it cannot be true always. The sense of 'to feel' as applied to emotions is discussed at greater length in Chapter 7.
2. The reality of the felt charge that belongs to much emotion and its distinctness from the other elements of emotion may be appreciated from a type of case in which it is conspicuously wanting, perversely in light of the setting (including the person's judgements): 'When the news of the death of his very dearly loved mother reached him in a distant city, he departed at once to the funeral. He was possessed by tormenting indifference despite all efforts to bring forth some feeling.' In another example, a man 'comes home to find a telegram saying his mother died and puts it on the table saying,

"Oh what a shock this'll be in the morning!" ' (Sashin, 1993) In introducing these materials, Sashin (of the Harvard Medical School) writes, 'When I say affect tolerance, what do I mean by affect? I mean subjectively felt feelings. And what is the ability to experience and tolerate affect? I mean the ability to respond to a stimulus which we would ordinarily expect to evoke feelings, such as would a surgical operation, a school exam or a death of a loved one, with feelings . . . Some people don't have the ability to feel feelings' (Ibid., p. 122).

3. Of course, desires can be tangible and lively – obtrusively present in the moment – as well as dispositional. One can ache with them. But this is just to say they are felt, and whether one subsumes these under the heading of emotion or sees them as an extra-emotional sphere of feeling, like bodily sensation, matters little.

4. It is tempting to view association and symbolism in particular as trading on beliefs, but this would be wrong. As we saw when discussing ritual in Chapter 2, my association of A with B may retain its sway without supposing for one minute that A is B (or even construing A as B). It is not always easy to say just what a symbol symbolises and replace the symbol with that description and capture its power via the substituted description.

5. Bedford (1956), p. 119.

6. Kenny (1963), p. 70.

CHAPTER 5

Heartfelt Thoughts

Certainly affective feelings are not beliefs, but it does not follow
that they are irreducible to any kind of cognitive process.
Armon-Jones, *Varieties of Affect*[1]

It should be apparent now that a plausible conception of emotion must
allow emotional feeling a salience it has not recently enjoyed in philosophy. It is what seems to distance emotion from thought, as something
larger. We have seen that by being *felt*, an emotion acquires properties
the thoughts pertaining to it do not have – One might say, the project
of elimination has failed. Yet this does not make felt emotion something
altogether different from thinking certain thoughts (as dizziness or tired-
ness are). For, the thrust of the preceding arguments has been, in effect,
that emotions, as felt, may stand in contrast with the *content* of one's
thoughts (so that a pessimistic outlook, for instance, needn't betoken
inward gloom). However, a sophisticated view of cognition needs wider
horizons. The import of a thought depends not just on its sense but on
its psychological context (Nussbaum's account traded on this general
fact). Roughly, a thought takes colour from the background of attitudes
that address it. Whether the thought of X strikes me like the stroke of
doom is a matter of how I am prepared to receive X-like prospects.
Perhaps it is as objects of certain attitudes that thoughts lie at the
heart of emotional arousal. In other words, perhaps emotional feelings
themselves are thoughts, emotive thoughts, transfigured in the right way.
(Reduction, one might say, may yet prevail.)

Arousal, indeed, is one irremovable feature of feeling. Perhaps for the
heart to open to a perception or thought – for the person to feel its force
or be affected by it – depends not just on the content of the thought or
perception but on the person's relation to that content. There are two
prominent attempts in modern philosophy to carry out this programme.
By purporting to capture affect – what it might be for a cognition to be
moving – they represent the final refinement of the cognitive approach
to emotion.

The most influential of these theories trades on the hedonic resonance the thoughts have with the person. I shall dub this the hedonic-cognitive theory. The other, notably subtle, approach trades on the power of care to inject aspectual meaning into experience; and I will call it the construal theory. Though proposed independently, these approaches to the problem of emotional affect or feeling are not as different as they seem. In this chapter I seek to assess the merits of each and of the strategy that unites them.

– THE FIRST MODEL –

The hedonic-cognitive theory is conveyed succinctly by Malcolm Budd's claim that, typically, an emotion is 'a thought experienced with pain or pleasure'.[2] But the most extended statement of it is found in Patricia Greenspan's book *Emotions and Reasons*. An emotion, Greenspan contends, comprises two elements: an evaluative component, which is a thought (this may or may not amount to outright belief), and an affective component, which is the comfort or discomfort taken in the thought. In a word, emotions 'are conceived as comfort or discomfort directed towards evaluative propositions'.[3] This offers to account for both the cognitive specifications that serve to identify the emotion and the element of arousal that we call having feelings of that emotion. 'The varieties of fear', for instance, 'seem to be relatively easily summed up in general . . . as involving discomfort at the thought that some form of injury is likely' (to oneself or to one's interests).[4] This means that an emotion has an internal object as well as an external object. Thus,

> In standard cases of emotion, on my view, there are two layers of intentionality, with the second seen as adding something more specific than the first. First, the affective component, comfort or discomfort, has an evaluative proposition as its object. This is what is referred to as an internal object 'of' the emotion, meaning an object of feeling internal *to* it. Secondly, the evaluative component of emotion, the proposition that *amounts to* its internal object, itself has an object, in the sense of something that it is about. This is taken as the external object of the emotion as a whole.[5]

Among the advantages of this theory are that it allows for emotions that are not directed at any external object, for example, some moods or emotions stirred by what is merely imagined. Similarly, it also allows emotions to involve thoughts about external objects that are not judgements about them. And in particular, it promises a place for the dimension of arousal or affect in emotion in the shape of a positive or negative response to the evaluative thought and can cope to that extent with the feature of (changeable) intensity that emotions have. Notice, too, that *valuation* seems to occur twice over, once as a valuational thought and again as one's satisfaction or dissatisfaction with this thought (and it will occur three times over if there can be the differences between valuational *thoughts* and value – *judgements* about the same thing noted above).

This compound structure to emotive valuation invites the question whether the feeling (that is, hedonic charge) and the appraising thought have to pull together. If they do not, then the possibilities for complexity amongst my valuation attitudes must be very great. This is especially so given the possibility of reflective emotions. I could warm to something I deplore (for example, blood sports), recoil at myself for this, then take comfort in the probity of at least *that* reaction. If all this is possible, if the psychology can be that complex, then the hedonic-cognitive theory is well suited to the ordeal of explaining it.

A complexity for which Greenspan explicitly provides is ambiguity of feeling. Someone subject to states of manic activity 'might come to see that his aroused state also had a *feverish* quality, unpleasant at the time, though he was then unaware of its unpleasant aspect.'[6] Emotions often involve 'affective mixture: comfort laced with, or layered over, discomfort. For even many genuinely pleasurable emotions, such as thrilled anticipation, do not amount to pure states of comfort . . . pleasurable emotional arousal, to the extent that it involves some *striving*, involves *both* comfort and discomfort.'[7] So, emotions do not just divide here between a simple positive or negative.[8]

– FIRST PROBLEM: HEDONIC TONE –

How successful is the hedonic-cognitive conception of the nature of emotional affect? An obvious question is whether feelings have to register hedonically at all. The fact that so many feelings plainly do is likely to obscure the question whether they must. Can a state be one of aroused feeling without being particularly agreeable or disagreeable? It does not seem impossible that an affective reaction should be keen and yet, at least in the moment, hedonically neutral. An example would be just feeling weird, being *impressed* by the strangeness of an utterly novel experience. I do not mean the alarming uncanniness or the exotic thrill that the strange can have, but a sheer, uncommitted, interrogative weirdness of which it is also capable – exciting but undecided as between the welcome and the unwelcome. Often the response to the new *is* hedonic and more or less foreordained by creaturely dispositions, as in a first experience of bereavement, being rescued from danger, being raped or being hunted. But sometimes nothing prepares a person for what awaits him on the far side of his present experiential horizons. Examples of first-time experiences that could be like this are: waking up on the high seas, weightlessness, committing a crime, going into battle, having sex or undergoing a rite of passage. Obviously some of the feelings here would be sensory or perceptual rather than emotive. Moreover, the initiate's *emotion* might even be in suspension, holding fire as, all attention, he absorbs what is happening, like a disengaged bystander. To be astonished, dazed, at a loss, bemused or just excited are, however, felt responses, states over and above vacant transparency to what is unfolding and the sensations of it. But there seems no necessity that they always be either agreeable or disagreeable, though they may become so.

How significant is the possibility of such cases? Given that 'emotions' do not constitute a sharply demarcated natural kind, a theory may hope to do justice to paradigmatic types (and tokens) of emotion and to the broader range of what we regard as emotions without having to cope with every marginal case. The possibility of experiences that are affectively charged yet hedonically uncommitted does demonstrate, however, that affective complexion does not consist just in hedonic tone. And that already exposes *a* shortfall in the hedonic-cognitive theory.

Perhaps this just warns us against expecting a general account of affect. For hedonic tone might be the form taken by affective charge in those cases where both of these are present. And since emotions typically, at least, do have hedonic weight, it would remain the primary form taken by emotive affect even if not its only possible form; and the latter fact then loses much of its interest.

Unfortunately, this offers to dispel the problem only by oversimplifying it. It is true that the agreeableness or disagreeableness that attaches to most emotions (whether as types or tokens) is a salient affective dimension of them. But even where present, these needn't exhaust the emotions full affective profile and cannot, indeed, always account for it. For the fact that there can be emotion which does not importantly involve pain or pleasure points to the fact that, even where these are present, the affective aspect of the emotion – may not depend on them. Thus, amongst feelings that *are* hedonically tinged, those weighted in the same direction can show contrasts that are not merely of degree. Tranquillity and relief may or may not be milder satisfactions than rapture or ecstasy; but quite apart from that, they are easeful rather than quickened experiences.

That the hedonic tone of an emotion may not exhaust its affective cast can be a quite important fact about it. For the latter, as distinct from the former, can be what actually differentiates emotive feelings. It is true that these feelings can remain comparatively vague and unresolved. I could be just upset generally at finding some shabby trait in myself; but my distress could also take finer forms: I could feel, variously, shocked, disappointed, depressed, grim or resigned (these could be phases through which my distress slowly passed). It is not clear that differences such as these can be captured as differences between discomfort and comfort, pain/pleasure or between varying degrees and mixtures of those. (Need these reactions, for their part, differ in level of discomfort at all?) In particular, it may fall to the experiential character of the feeling to qualify its hedonic tone, that is, to account for how it is agreeable or disagreeable as distinct from how agreeable or disagreeable it is. Certainly, such shadings are to be found. As Aaron Ridley observes,

> In certain cases the substitution of other hedonic tone words will distort, or miss, the character of the emotion in question. 'Acute distress at the thought of the death of someone who is dear to one' is a formulation to which grief will conform. But 'acute dissatisfaction at the thought of the death of someone who is dear to one' is not. No doubt there is some murky state of mind thus to be captured; but it is not grief. And nor is grief an exception in this context. Consider joy described in terms of extreme comfort, or love in terms of satisfaction (or even of pleasure). So it seems that emotions involve different hedonic tones (different 'kinds of pleasure and pain') and that these tones differ not simply with respect to their positive and negative characters.[9]

And, indeed, pleasures and displeasures do come in a host of forms. However, it would be a mistake to infer from this that pleasure and its opposite are *themselves* kinds of experience which happen to accompany others. The sort of pleasure one has must depend on what it is a pleasure in, the kind of comfortlessness on what is comfortless, and so on.

A hedonic-cognitive theory, must, therefore, seek affective differences in contrasts amongst the *thoughts* at which the binary affective pulses are directed.[10] On this theory, distinctions of feeling will have to be firmly rooted in differences in propositional content (not in their phenomenology, for instance).

– SECOND PROBLEM: THE DEFINING THOUGHTS –

Can the element of valuational thought hope to bear this burden? A prerequisite for this, of course, is that there should always *be* a thought of a suitable form. Yet finding the right valuational thought is not always a straightforward matter. Proponents of the hedonic-cognitive theory urge that the thought that gives shape to a person's feeling need not be formulated and explicit. Greenspan holds that 'the "thought" in my analysis pattern need not be explicitly entertained', and Budd speaks of it as capable of being 'conveyed or embodied in an experience'.[11] When we consider emotions as types, the kinds of thought that would or could severally make for them are often (if not always) clear enough. When we come to tokens or specific occurrences of these emotions, however, actual realisations of these thoughts can be hard to find. Thoughts of the sorts that could be the focus of episodes of a given emotion are not always their focus. Unfortunately we are not free to ascribe to someone just any thought that might make sense of his reaction. If a valuational thought is to be an *intentional* object of what one feels, one must be responding to it as such, that is, *as* a valuational thought or propositional content. To be the thought that actually inspired the person's feeling, it must, presumably at least, be accessible to that person and subject to certain constraints: it must have been occurrent (that is, not just a thought he might or would have had but didn't), and it must be something he could formulate and would recognise not just as apt but as his own and as the actual basis of his response. Interpretation must not just confabulate. As a case of a feeling that encompasses a thought, the following (from Nelson Mandela's autobiography) is as promising a candidate as any:

> no one ever walked through [Dr Wellington's door] except Dr Wellington himself. Suddenly, the door opened and out walked not Dr Wellington, but a black man dressed in a leopard-skin kaross and matching hat who was carrying a spear in either hand . . . the sight of a black man in tribal dress coming through the door was electrifying. It is hard to explain the impact it had on us. It seemed to turn the universe upside down.[12]

Notice, however, that the specific focus of the excitement here is on the actual moral universe and the seeming inversion of it that occurred then rather than on a *proposition* (or even thought) about it. The general thought, or proposition, that the moral universe is thus changeable is more a reflection that this experience might precipitate and which might ensue on the excitement of the moment, prompted by it and then supervene on the development of the experience – naturally, the reaction is to some aspect that the world is taken to present. However, to rejoice in the world that appears in a certain way is not the same as rejoicing in the *description* of the world as so appearing (and that, in turn, needn't be the same as rejoicing that the world can be described thus). Mandela's description of his astonishment all those years ago as being at the overturning of the moral universe is doubtless apt, but it is formulated here in retrospect and there is no reason to suppose that the young Mandela was even capable of forming this thought at the time.

To appreciate this, it is worth noting cases in which the focus *is* on a particular description or way of thinking of something – the presentation as distinct from the presented. I may be uncomfortable with a thought for its properties as a thought, for example, just because it crowds out all others and obsesses me. Mere images can disturb ('The mere *thought* of a child's death disturbs me' – where there is no actual threat of this). I may ply myself with reassuring thoughts to calm myself, as I might seek soothing words, without reference to their veracity. Again, a thought may please because it is, to me, a novel, exotic, imaginative thought that represents an achievement, or because it is the correct answer in a quiz, however little I care what it is about. So an affective response can indeed be directed specifically at the thoughts that are had, but this seems a rather special subject of concern rather than the paradigmatic one. That I react to things only as thought of in a certain way does not mean that I am reacting to my thinking of them in that way. A thought as an internal object of a feeling marks an unusual case, not the usual one.

However, if feelings are only occasionally *about* thoughts, mustn't they still occur *through* them? If it is something in the world that characteristically arouses us, is this not the world as described or conceived in certain terms? And if we are moved by things only as they appear to us under this or that aspect, won't the delineation of that aspect be the specification of our feeling? Surely, it might seem, the nature of the feeling resides in how the thing attracting it is thought of.

Closely examined, this is less persuasive than it sounds. If thoughts are what characterises feelings and differentiates them, then it should be impossible for two people to differ in positive or in negative reactions to the same thought. The following should not be able to happen: what disgusts Jack, but without frightening him (for example, discovering or thinking of a slug in the pantry), frightens Jill but without disgusting her. But this does not seem impossible. Obviously, such a difference of response could result from an aspectual difference in the respective perceptions.

For instance, what is perceived as polluting by Jack (thus disgusting him) is perceived as threatening by Jill (thus frightening her). But it is doubtful whether this kind of helpful explanatory aspectual loading to the perception is always available at the time or, accordingly, that it is always necessary for the reaction to be as it is. For notice that the aspectual terms mentioned above only abbreviate the thoughts that would supposedly account for the contrasting affective reactions. A Diesel oil stain would *pollute* at least as much, yet without the distinctive ghastliness. So is it the eruption of Nature into Civilisation (the Raw lurking in the Cooked) that is the specific form of pollution here and the heart of the disgust? Then why is a creeping, animate intrusion worse than a seeping inanimate one? We must refine further(!) As to the *danger* that presents itself to Jill, surely a spill of inflammable liquid would be a clearer and graver danger. So to explain what makes *this* fear so jolting or chilling, the description must again be amplified and made more subtle and searching. Realistic specification of the thoughts that would ground a reaction and furnish it with an intelligible content can prove a disarming challenge, even in simple and familiar cases.

As the case of Mandela's amazement suggests, however, the proposition that would make sense of an affective response *can* emerge (perhaps with difficulty) only on reflection, without figuring in the thoughts or perceptions of the moment. That a certain thought nicely describes an affective state does not make it the content of that state. Feelings can be conspicuously unperspicuous as to their grounds and causes. The aspect of a thing under which it could explain my response to it need not be an aspect under which I then apprehend it, even tacitly. Even where fully characterising thoughts *do* attend the feelings or can be teased out (that is, are tacit), they are apt to be incomplete as explications. Thus, thoughts that succeed in pinpointing the evocative aspects of a thing tend to do so simply by referring to their power to evoke the feeling in question: cute, sweet, lovely, delicious, grim, looming – and, in Jack's case, repellent. We recoil not at the viscous or glassy or slithery as such but at the repellently glassy or viscous or slithery, and that reaction remains, to an extent, potent to us.

Admittedly, many reactions do have grounds that are independent of them and that fall within the individual's experience. Even these, however, as thoughts, needn't belong to the content of the reaction and may serve only as part of its causal background. A woman who lived through repeated bombing raids in the last war finds herself distressed by the rumbling sound made by the trams in the street below her flat, to the extent that she eventually has to move. What distressed her? There are at least two distinct possibilities: (1) she identified the tram sound with the drone of incoming bombers, in that as a tram drew closer, she found herself hearing the sound of approaching bomber formations again and felt the old dread. But there is no need for this to happen. The past can prepare one for the present less cumbersomely: (2) the tram sound could stir dread in her directly and immediately, without any such harkening back. A tram sound just is strangely upsetting to her. This could be because the droning of bombers disposed her to these later reactions without obtruding into them. After all, places, even sights, sounds or aromas often have an atmosphere, an affective cast, to a person whose poignancy is as clear as its origins are obscure, then or perhaps forever. Reverberations needn't be self-diagnosing.

So if it is true that the world quickens feeling in a person only under some aspect that it has for him, the only description he may have of that aspect, if he has one at all, may be in terms of affective properties. In the moment, the sight of the black man in Dr Wellington's doorway was amazing, releasing; the slug alarming or disgusting; the tram rumble unnerving.

The hedonic-cognitive theory, a prevailing way of trying to understand the element of feeling in emotions cognitively, is, then, unsuccessful. Affective arousal is not confined to the binary or to the hedonic. The spectrum of feeling is not restricted to light and dark. And any thoughts through which the objects of feeling may be presented may just refer us back to the feelings themselves.

The *affective* tone and charge that so often mark emotion cannot lie in the affected person's attitude to thoughts that might occur to him. After all, there may be none. Presumably, non-linguistic creatures such as infants and animals, who are incapable of articulated thought, are accessible to at least some kinds of emotion. A successful account of what it means to be so affected must be able to allow for that.[13]

– THE SECOND MODEL: THE LOOK OF THINGS –

Cognition might remain at the centre of even creaturely affect if cognition can take non-propositional forms. Robert Roberts has developed a theory of the emotions which permits this.[14] It purports to show how the capacity for emotion (and some specific types of emotion) can be common to animals and adult humans. Our question is whether it shows that emotive affect is a form of cognition even when distinct from thought. Roberts draws attention to the role of what he calls 'construal', typified by the aspectual character of perception, which he thinks creatures incapable of forming or formulating thoughts share with those that are.[15] My cat's stare, which looks cute to me, may look ominous to a rabbit. And its menacing appearance to the rabbit needn't (perhaps can't) owe to mediating speculations on the rabbit's part about the predator's intentions or to images of being eaten (that is, to thoughts about the situation). And we ourselves retain this primitive susceptibility. Even for discursive minds, the evocativeness of something may depend on its 'aspectual shape',[16] rather than on a formulatable description or assessment (or as well as that). I, too, could be unnerved *just* by the predator's stare as distinct from what I know or imagine it to portend (or by both). This permits a complex cognitive layering in mature humans. There can be different aspects of the same thing, one formulatable, one not and one emotively evocative and the other not: a body may not look to the medical eye as it does to the erotic eye (even if the eye is the same). Also, aspectual characterisation can be assertional as well as perceptual, imputed and entertained as well as just seen. I may believe the defendant guilty and a villain or I may *accept* (*believe*) that he is guilty but, despite everything, still *picture* him as an innocent, owing to the bewildered *look* in his eyes.

Emotion, however, requires more than just aspectual characterisation, as Roberts himself stresses. Aspectual shape needn't be emotively provocative at all; and when it is, it underdetermines emotive response. The lion's stare may well look to me full of menacing intent, but I contemplate it tranquilly from my sturdy vehicle. The beholder *can* see, and appreciate, a body erotically without actually delighting in it or being thrilled by it (he might recoil puritanically or just be too tired to react).

So construal can be a primordial, pre-discursive form of cognition which survives in mature adults, but its power to insinuate itself into the emotional life requires more. This Roberts duly supplies. Emotion, he suggests, takes its rise out of the *concern* that enters into the subject's construal: 'For anger to be generated, the concern not to be insulted has to qualify the perception of the insult; the perception of the insult has to impinge on the concern; the concern has to be a "term" of the construal.'[17] So, for instance, 'My view of that interviewer as powerful and contemptuous gives her a threatening look only if filtered through my concern to succeed.'[18] An emotion, then, is a construal structured by a concern. An aspect will be alarming, delightful, aggravating, and so on, depending on what one cares about.

How, exactly, is *concern* to be understood here? (Roberts himself speaks of it both as the basis of construals and as a 'term' of them.[19]) They are supposed to include 'desires and aversions, and the attachments and interests from which many of our desires and aversions derive'.[20] Now whatever else it may be,[21] a concern that stirs me out of neutrality is surely a susceptibility to react contentedly or discontentedly to certain things, to be gratified or discomfited by them. Care, of whatever kind, turns events into a drama of welcome or unwelcome fortune. Yet notice that emotion conceived as a pro- or con- reaction to a given presentation of something is not so very different from emotion conceived as thought of something in which pleasure or pain is had. The concerned construal conception of emotion can be seen as an extended version of the hedonic-cognitive theory. For if it is as a susceptibility to satisfaction or dissatisfaction that a concern is the source of my affective stirrings, then the only difference between the theories is that the concerned construal theory has a broader perspective on the kinds of cognition emotions can involve. This is a gain, but it still rests emotions on binary hedonic attitudes.

Now, concerns, in their turn, can be more than binary. They are richer than this precisely where the susceptibilities they represent (the ways I care) show themselves in the ways things arouse me and reside in these. But this is an appeal to the character of different kinds of emotional arousal to understand the nature of concern. (Adoration gets me to see the baby's gestures as cute rather than clumsy; anxiety gets me to see impending calamity everywhere; adoration and anxiety are concerns, but they are also emotions.) Recall that in discussing the hedonic-cognitive theory, we were driven to appeal to terms for emotive affect to describe adequately the kinds of thought that identify and distinguish the varieties of emotion (disgusting, looming, lovely). The same happens here.

However, the problem left by these theories is not just one of circularity. There is a further problem (which will combine with the first to form a dilemma). Notice that a person's emotional response cannot be downright *inferred* from the nature of the concerned perception they have of their situation (and so cannot be assimilated to that). Uncle Julius sees his generosity as having been taken for granted and abused – perhaps other constructions could be put on the same events, but this is what he makes of them. And he cares: he doesn't just *believe* he has been treated shabbily, he feels used.[22] This is his concerned construal of his situation.[23] (In the terms of the hedonic-cognitive theory, he finds the thought that he has been taken for granted displeasing.) Actually, however, none of this need yet be his emotion or even decide it. A certain psychological distance still separates feeling used (*and* minding that) from the fully resolved affective responses to which such frames of mind open him, of which more than one is possible. Feeling used and caring about it, he might give way to resentment, out of which bitterness might grow (or not); but he might be more hurt than angered or be just saddened by it all; again, he might be resigned – not detached from his treatment or insensitive to it but not provoked by it either.

Such possibilities are easily concealed by the fact that often, especially in simple stereotypical cases, the affective impact of a concerned construal (or hedonically toned thought) *is* immediate and assured. An anxious person who sees something as a threat is pretty well going to fear it. Again, some forms of affective arousal (for example, anger, joy, fear) just are ways of minding about things. But the intimacy of many concerned construals with affective states should not obscure the degree of indeterminacy there can also be in their relations. There is an uncertainty to the movements of emotive feeling that lends to the life of the emotions much of its chanciness. My care-imbued perception certainly does prefigure the form of my arousal. The content of this perception establishes the general type of the emotion (for example, as 'not best pleased') and gives it reference, the intentionality an emotion needs; but it can do this without pre-ordaining the precise form of the sentiment.

Now, this is not an obvious claim. For clearly there are apprehensions specifically appropriate, respectively, to anger, to resentment, to bitterness, to sadness and to the other kinds of discomfiture – proprietary perceptions that *can* distinguish each from the others (in sadness the focus of concern is on loss rather than on outrageousness, as in anger, or on loss to *me*, as in hurt, and so forth). And the focus of one's care amongst these considerations could indeed decide one's specific emotion. Notice, however, that even if apprehending something in a given care-imbued aspectual shape is tantamount to proprietary emotive response, the converse does not follow – it does not follow that a response signals full proprietary aspectual shape to the one who responds. Now, this is apt to be concealed by the fact that if someone responds affectively to things in a certain way, they do *acquire* a distinctive aspectual shape to him. But even if the emotion would rise out of the construal and the construal out of the emotion, it does not follow that the emotion does rise, fully formed, from the construal. And in practice, the answer to the question 'How does that (that is, your situation as you construe it) leave you feeling?' is not always foregone. An arousal of emotion needn't await the resolution and precision of perception that would make sense of (and could evoke) it. The passage from preparatory cognitive background to response can be abrupt rather than mediated by suitably informing thoughts. How we will feel may be unclear until we feel it and may not be a perspicuous response even then: it may surprise, intrigue or shock ('It affected me strangely'). We are, in the revealing phrase, 'overtaken' by our emotion.

Some will be tempted by an alternative to this account of what happens when an emotion seems to overtake us, one that would preserve precision of match between concerned construal and evoked feeling. This is that we do not know our own mind at the time, and our emotion is the sole clue to it. That is, we *are* possessed of a conceptualisation that we do not recognise and that surfaces initially in the form of emotion. We discussed the appeal to tacit and unconscious thoughts in Chapter 2. Suffice it to say here that to postulate unheralded proprietary conceptualisation or even construal wherever 'out of the way' emotion occurs is to invoke mental structure prescriptively and unnecessarily. The dawning of aspectual shape could arise, as in the Mandela example above, through and from the emotion rather than realise itself in it. Moreover, it is not impossible for the well of construal to go dry: one may, even on reflection, actually find nothing to invite the emotion, so that it strikes one as wayward.

Allowing for a gap between preliminary construal and actual emotive response is the simplest way to make sense of reports of the form, 'I can't get over *how* bad it is' or 'I wasn't prepared for it to be like *this*', where 'it' refers to one's state of feeling.

The point of showing indeterminacy to be possible between how one construes a situation and how it affects one is not just to tease out some exceptions to what is otherwise the rule. The lesson of the fact that familiar types of emotion can be undergone where construals specific to them are lacking is wider. It is that even in the paradigmatic cases, where proprietary construals are present at the inception and in the content of the emotion, they are not all there is to it.

Nor does the claim that how a person feels may be a step beyond how he thinks make the former mysterious. That the source of an emotion is not wholly evident from its internal structure does not make it arbitrary. Features of the person's temperament generally (thin-skinned, phlegmatic, sensitive) or current frame of mind (worked up, vulnerable, tense) can contribute to the tilt of their affective dispositions. Of course temperament and momentary state of mind include cognitive traits ('mind sets'), such as optimism, trustingness, insecurity or poor self-esteem. However, it would be arbitrary to maintain that all the dispositions of temperament can only make themselves felt *via* these and never directly. Temperament and state of mind also include concerns; and an emotional state is a concerned state (not one of indifference). Again, however, to be specific enough to match precisely the way one feels (and not to leave that in some measure indeterminate), a concern may have to be specified in terms of that feeling – as a disposition to it. Then, to call an emotion a concerned construal becomes unilluminating.[24]

The following poem by Emily Dickenson brings these points into relief:

> There's a certain slant of
> light,
> on winter afternoons.
> That oppresses, like the
> weight
> of cathedral tunes.

Clearly (1) the look of that wintery light does not by itself determine that we should find it oppressive (the response is not inevitable); and (2) the sort of slant that is oppressive is only apparent when we become oppressed by it. The concern touched by such light (assuming the notion of a concern has any purchase here) can only be the concern that light should become tenuous in *that* way, the way that oppresses.

The dilemma, then, is this: concerns that are *precisely* enough embodied in how we feel to perfectly specify it have themselves to be specified in terms of that and so do not illuminate the nature of emotive arousal. On the other hand, concerns specifiable in terms other than of how we feel prefigure the feelings but fall short of them. Where it is not vacuous, then, this theory, like the hedonic-cognitive theory, is incomplete.

Each of the two theories considered here presents emotional affect as cognition suitably qualified. And they must solve the problem set by this 'cognition +'[25] approach (namely, of what distinguishes those thoughts or perceptions that 'get to us') in the same way: we are affectively stirred by the aspects of things that agree or disagree with us – otherwise they do not touch our concern, and we remain detached, at least emotionally. When applied to how we feel in particular cases, however, this consideration is either true but too unspecific or true by importing an antecedent understanding of the affective complexion of the experience at hand. What the latter, our feeling, is remains unaccounted for, save that it amounts to more than these theories have to offer.

Where does this leave the philosophy of emotion? Still up in the air. We do learn something valuable about the emotionally aroused frame of mind, but not what is emotive about it. The two theories (the Theory?) examined here are among the most recent and subtle attempts to shed light on precisely this. Another approach is needed.

– NOTES –

1. Armon-Jones (1991), p. 28.
2. Budd (1985), pp. 5 and 129.
3. Greenspan (1988), p. 14.
4. Ibid., p. 15.
5. Ibid., p. 16.
6. Ibid., p. 30.
7. Ibid., p. 31.
8. We are not told, however, whether the very same thought is invested with both positive and negative affect or whether these attach to the external object regarded under different aspects, via different thoughts, which would actually yield two emotions, positive and negative, rather than one that is both. Notice that this would mean that there *is* a simple division of emotions into positive and negative.
9. Ridley (1995), pp. 24–5.
10. It seems inadvisable to say, as some have, that the hedonic character of a feeling is determined by the 'concept' of the emotion in question, e.g. by whether it rates as anger, embarrassment or shame – do we actually have a concept for everything we feel? And as with tastes, our powers to formulate apt descriptions may outrun our modest and often roughcast fixed typology.
11. Greenspan, (1988), p. 21 and Budd (1985), p.13.
12. Nelson Mandela (1995), p. 48.
13. Deigh (1994).
14. Roberts (1996).
15. Roberts (1988), pp. 190–5; Roberts (1996), pp. 148–50.
16. This term is drawn from Searle (1995), p. 131, in his discussion of intentionality.
17. Roberts (1996), p. 150.
18. Roberts (1988), p. 192.
19. Roberts (1996), p. 150.
20. Roberts (1988), p. 202.
21. Where they are desires, the concerns formative of emotions and their attendant construals would seem to belong more to the explanation of emotional reactions than to their composition. If so, emotions would be 'based' on them primarily in a causal sense. In several ways, emotions do seem distinct from desires. I will not enlarge on this claim here, but see the discussion in Stocker (1983), pp. 10–18 and above pp. 48–53.
22. Feeling used is not yet an instance of an emotion. 'Feel' serves here to designate, rather more widely, how one perceives one's condition and what perceiving that is like. This is certainly apt to include at least dispositions to affective responses but it need not do so. Thus, when I announce that I feel free at last, it makes sense to ask, 'And how does *that* make you feel?' And here the focus *is* on emotion or its quality: feeling free, I might feel exhilarated or frightened or both or neither.
23. Such a situation admits of more specific construals: I might be particularly mindful

of the effort I had gone to which is now treated so obliviously; I might focus on the ingrate's undeservingness of such efforts in the first place, and there are other possibilities. The circumstances might also be more complicated than those I describe in this example. However, it seems perfectly possible for a construal to occur in no more developed a form than I describe and for that to impinge on me emotionally in a narrow range of not fully predictable ways.

24. If the concern for, say, face, just amounted to the disposition to shame at certain things, then to say shame is a construal shaped by this concern is to say shame reflects the disposition to shame.

25. An expression I owe to A. Ridley.

CHAPTER 6

The Subjectivity of Feeling

It would be difficult to exaggerate the disastrous effects that the failure to come to terms with the subjectivity of consciousness has had on the philosophical and psychological work of the past half century.

John Searle, *The Rediscovery of the Mind*

– CROSS-ROADS –

We have found emotions to be miscast without feeling and feeling to be miscast in terms of thoughts, even those shaped and hedonically enlivened by one's concerns, rudimentarily affective though these are. To do justice to both the nature and the role of feeling we must pass from cognitive maximalism, even in its more refined incarnations, and lay the ground for a cognitively minimalist approach.

– FEELING AND SUBJECTIVITY –

In the passages cited from Styron's *Darkness Visible* in Chapter 4, the emotions undergone in the course of depression were, crucially, states of feeling (the *anguish* of the 'despair beyond despair'). What these feelings are is above all a matter of how feeling them feels (the 'sensation close to, but indescribably different from, actual pain'[1]) that is, of their experienced character.

To accommodate this often vital and sometimes defining feature of emotions, it is necessary to take seriously the notion of the subjective tone or complexion that an experience may have, in which feeling, we must now suspect, in large part consists.

– DEFINING SUBJECTIVITY –

Now, just what is subjectivity? The concept is anything but straight-forward. On the one hand, it seems *prima facie* an essential feature of feelings; on the other, however, it is neither intuitively nor theoretically clear enough a notion to be used without further ado. It is ignored in some quarters and contested in others. In many, it stirs deeply nurtured philosophical and methodological fears.

The founding attempt to make an honest concept of subjectivity was by Thomas Nagel in his two papers 'What is it Like to be a Bat?' and 'Subjective and Objective'.[2] He claimed that subjectivity is what distinguishes states as conscious or as experiences, and tried to delineate subjectivity in a well-known phrase: 'an organism has conscious mental states if and only if there is something it is like to *be* that organism – something it is like *for* the organism.'[3] This condition of being host to conscious experience is explained as the organism's having a point of view on the world, a point of view which is its own and nothing else's, however much or little the world as disclosed through it resembles what emerges from other points of view.

There has been a confusion of responses from philosophers to subjectivity so understood. Some accept it without demur as an obvious and vital part of the life of some minds, whilst others dismiss it either as a resurrection of the discredited idea of epistemological privacy, notwithstanding Nagel's protest to the contrary, or as a piece of prescientific mystification. Robust hostiles include Kathleen Wilkes:

> I would deny that I know what it is like to be me, or human, or female . . . A more direct objection is to query the coherence of the postulation of such puzzling facts. Thus to object would be to marshal some of the familiar arguments against the 'myth of the given', or against the view that there can indeed be knowledge-by-acquaintance which is *not* knowledge by (or under) a description; it challenges the idea that facts can be ineffable even though nonconceptually effed by their possessor. If the Wittgensteinian-cum-Strawsonian arguments against the presuppositions of a private language go through, the subject cannot create *a novo* a subjective phenomenology for himself . . .[4]

and more recently, Daniel Dennett:

> The structure of a bat's mind is just as accessible as the structure of a bat's digestive system; the way to investigate either one is to go back and forth systematically between an assay of its contents and an assay of the world from which its contents were derived, paying attention to the methods and goals of the derivation.[5]

On the other hand, at the very time of Wilkes' pronouncement, Wollheim declared: 'As for showing that there is no such thing as subjectivity, I can conceive of nothing that we could do or say that might be expected to serve this purpose.'[6] And not long after Dennett's attempt to do just that, John Searle urged on us 'a world picture that contains subjectivity as a rock-bottom element'.[7]

Clearly, the notion of the subjectivity of experience is not to be employed casually.

– DOUBTING SUBJECTIVITY –

The standard criticism of the whole notion that experience can have a subjective dimension – represented by Wilkes, Dennett and others – assumes that a subjective state is a kind of *knowledge*, that my point of view (the one that is no one else's) resolves itself into something that only I know. So interpreted, the idea invites two familiar lines of attack. The first is on the possibility of epistemological privacy. And the second is on the inaccessibility of my supposed privileged knowledge. Both attacks are quite beside the point.

The first, which has the bulk of a whole philosophical tradition behind it, will be examined in the next chapter. The second, typified by the passage from Dennett quoted earlier, tries to show that we can after all reconstruct the 'contents of a creature's mind' even where we cannot share its kind of experience (for example, perceptual stimuli). We can work out what facts the bat must register to be able to do what it does, for example, the location and velocity of flying insects and perhaps the nature of the representational matrix it uses for this if it is not the three-dimensional space of our own visual and tactual perception.

If the subjective quality of an experience consisted in the *knowledge* of what it was like, presumably it would take precisely the form of thought (normally propositional). But then in invoking it as a key notion in understanding emotive feeling, we would not have advanced beyond the approaches to this already surveyed and rejected. The question of the reducibility of subjectivity to a kind of knowledge therefore has a heavy bearing on the understanding of feeling.

Now, the subjective quality of my experience does seem precisely not to be a matter of the sort of thing I know but at most, perhaps, what the experiences are like that lead me to this knowledge. The fact that the sunlight makes me squint and put on dark glasses shows that I am light-sensitive (should the idiom be more informational: 'photocognizant'?); but that says nothing about what glare looks and feels like to such a sighted creature. This is easily missed in cases of perception (construal) and interpretation, for they are of necessity heavily informational, and their subjective aspects, such as they may be, are easily occluded. It is otherwise with feeling, however. You could determine what I know without securing knowledge of what I feel. Moreover, you can know what I feel whilst the experience of it remains foreign to you. Writing of the 'toxic and unnamable tide' of dysphoria that accompanies major depression, William Styron asserts that 'To most of those who have experienced it, the horror of depression is so overwhelming as to be quite beyond expression, hence the frustrated sense of inadequacy found in the work of even the greatest artists.'[8] It should be obvious that the dysphoria gestured at here is not the same as the realisation that these things are true of it. To feel an all-consuming melancholia is not to know these things about it so much as to be *in a position* to know them (authoritatively). And in some cases a person can have a feeling without *knowing* it (or anything about it). Subjective tone is not primarily a matter of first-personal knowledge. Thus what Dennett offers triumphantly to reconstruct, from however afar you please, isn't there.

These assertions may sound rushed. How safe are they on examination? Presumably I would have to think of what an experience is like in order to know I was having it. So if I cannot have it without knowing I have it (what I have), then, contrary to the argument above, I would indeed have to know what it was like to have it at all. Is this so? The challenging question, here, is whether experience can have a complexion (including an affective cast) to it of which the individual to whom it has this complexion is unaware. – For experience to be like something to me do I have to *know* what it is like? In particular, can I feel a certain way without *recognising* how I feel?

– SUBJECTIVITY AND WHAT YOU KNOW –

Consider the past and whether there can be something a person's circumstances were like to him without his realising it, especially whether the presence and nature of feelings can be apparent only retrospectively. It does seem that people can be depressed, invigorated, tense or serene without realising it. Depression, serenity, vigour and the like can manifest themselves all along in how the person experiences things without his recognising them for what they are. And these states need not be merely dispositional, that is, ways the person would react under given circumstances or patterns in what he does, to which he is oblivious. A child can delight in its play, even though it may not *think* of itself in these terms, either because it lacks the concept of delight or because it does not stop to reflect. The child may just 'live' the delight of the moment. Conversely, the possession of the concept and the habit of reflection by an adult can contribute simultaneously to misery and to his failure to recognise this. That is, furnished with both the conception of satisfaction as something to be sought and of what should yield it, someone who achieves what he thinks should yield it may mistake a persisting yearning and emptiness for a ringing call to work, a pervading restlessness for energy, an indifference to most things and people for contentment, and a proneness to moral aggression for a vibrant sense of fairness. Someone in any of these states is actively and palpably ill at ease in life. He is subject to the aggravation of a malaise the manifestations of which he cannot recognise because of his beliefs about himself and how life is to be led; and he is oblivious to this. Disquiet loses little by being misarticulated. And if it did, one's beliefs about oneself would become true merely by being believed and self-deceit would be the shortcut to perfection.

A person who is oblivious to his actual stirrings is different from the one in whom they are just unawakened. Ignorance of one's own serenity or disquiet is possible. Subjectivity need not be conceived as something reflexive, something which has to be recognised by the one whom it qualifies, in short as a kind of knowledge.

Now, if it is not properly regarded as a kind of knowledge at all, then it cannot be doubted for being a dubious kind of knowledge. The playing child does not even non-conceptually 'eff' that it is happy; nor is its delight dependent on any ability to frame a private language or consult a subjective phenomenology. Not even Nagel claimed that there is something which a bat *knows* it is like to be a bat.

To be sure, there can be facts about the subjective character of an experience that can be known, and known by others (who may even know more about them). A psychologist may know things about childhood fears or a torture victim's trauma that no child or victim knows (for example, facts about origins and prognosis); but there is also a sense in which the fear or trauma may be a closed world to the psychologist. What it is in states of emotional dislocation that can be closed to the professionally knowledgeable is precisely what they are like to those who are in them. Thus, Styron notes that many psychiatrists 'simply do not seem to be able to comprehend the nature and depth of the anguish their patients are undergoing'.[9]

It is even possible that most experience is adorned with subjective qualities that elude recognition almost all the time. This is brought out where these pervading characteristics of ordinary experience are disrupted. The psychoanalytic writer W. R. D. Fairbairn notes what he calls

> transient disturbances of the reality sense, e.g., feelings of 'artificiality' (whether referred to the self or the environment), experiences such as the 'plate glass feeling.' Feelings of unfamiliarity with familiar persons or environmental settings, and feelings of familiarity with the unfamiliar.[10]

One does not normally remark on feeling 'real', or on the accessibility of the immediate environment, or on the familiarity of the familiar (or the unfamiliarity of the unfamiliar). Only in their absence do these otherwise mute feelings first become conspicuous. 'Real,' accessible, familiar/unfamiliar are what certain things are like to me whether I realise it or not.

The fact that the subjective character of an experience needn't be reflexive undermines another major criticism of the whole concept.

– DEEPER DOUBTS? –

This more fundamental challenge to the whole notion of subjectivity is that it is logically unstable. Suppose my fingers grow numb with cold, muses Norman Malcolm:

> Won't there be a further question of 'what it was like for me' for my fingers to feel numb with cold? And what am I to say about that? . . . Nagel's use of these expressions is *regressive*: it has a constant backward movement [. . .] Given *any* experience, Nagel is saying, *that* experience too has a specific subjective character.[11]

(An analogous argument would be: 'Anything one can see has some chromatic tone or other. One of course sees the tone it has. Therefore chromatic tone must itself have a chromatic tone.') Two assumptions about the concept of subjectivity seem implicit here: (1) for any experience there is something that experience is like to the experiencer; (2) what an experience is like is an experience in its own right, distinct from any experience it qualifies. Now, (2), the imputation that the subjective character of an experience must be a piggyback response to it, is baseless. How something tastes does not have to be separate from its taste. A thrill *is* how it feels (what it is like), not something antecedent. What a feeling is like just determines the feeling it is. Of course, the *condition* of being ostracised or having frozen fingers is distinct from the *experience* of it, that is, from what it may be like to be in that condition; but the experience of being in that condition just is whatever it is like. 'Numb' says it all.

The same holds for elaborations on what an experience is like – the nuances of that – that go beyond merely labelling. Calling a fear abject or creeping, or one's delight astonished, answers – without reopening – the question of what it is like.

The fact that the subjective character of experiences can be thus self-contained allows them to be layered *without* generating a vicious regress. If an experience indeed does resonate subjectively in ways distinct from it ('I felt so relieved and found *that* so depressing'), no regress need develop. For, a resonance need resonate no further.

– How Feelings Are Subjective –

If it isn't obvious that there is something that emotional feeling is like, both as such and in its variegated forms, then the very contrast between apathy and passion, and changes from one kind of feeling to another (joy to sadness), should make it so. What is less obvious is the suggestion, developed above, that unreflected feeling is possible, that a period of life, even a whole life, can be suffused with a climate of feeling that is not recognised by its host. Let the following case serve as witness to both these facts:

> In retrospect, she said, she had been depleted of energy for as long as she could remember, had almost not known what it was to feel rested and hopeful. She had been depressed, it now seemed to her, her whole life. She was astonished at the sensation of being free of depression.[12]

However, the sense in which emotions can be (and emotional feelings are) subjective states is more complex than meets the eye. In the first place, there can be a difference between what feeling x (for example, sad or curious) is like and what it is like to feel it, a resonance that a given experience may or may not have, as noted in the last section. The latter encompasses the second-order feelings such as thrilled, startled, alarmed, relieved or ashamed, appalled, amused. These can be responses to how one initially feels. Now, feelings of both orders can contribute to what it is like to have a certain outlook on the world. After a landlocked childhood, a traveller catches his first sight of the ocean. He finds it more vast than he could have imagined, and purer, and more radiant than anything he has ever seen. That is how it is to him in this first moment, his outlook on it. As such, it astonishes and bedazzles him. This is how his outlook affects him, how it feels. But that, in its turn, leaves him feeling elevated and gladdened. This buoying up is how the primary feelings affect him, how it feels to undergo such feelings. (It is not inconceivable that there should be further ramifications of affect in this process, but the regress here is not vicious: it needn't get started and it can, and as a matter of psychological fact will, taper off before very many stages.) The feelings here seem to qualify, almost pre-eminently, as subjective phenomena, for it is quite impossible to conceive of them except in terms of what they are respectively like and what it is like to have them. Does this make them points of view on the world? Notice that they are not the same as the outlook, which could be a perception or characterising thought. The outlook ('vaster than I could have imagined') is a point of view on the world, whilst the feelings (bedazzled, gladdened, respectively) are what having that point of view is like, what this point of view arouses in the person. Really, then, Nagel's two criteria of subjectivity, point of view and what that point of view is like, part company.

This throws up a natural question. A feeling may not be the outlook that rouses us to it, but it can characterise that outlook. This is because the feeling itself can be characterised (disillusionment can be bitter, bittersweet or just sad). Even if a state of feeling is not the same as its description and need not be recognised to be undergone, feelings can be recognised and described, and they can be conveyed. How?

– APPENDIX
EMOTION WITHOUT SUBJECTIVITY: THE VIEW FROM PSYCHOLOGY –

It is possible to study emotion without reference to feeling. Indeed, in many intellectual traditions anything that smacks of subjectivity may fall victim not to neglect but to methodological exile, abandoned in favour of the aspects of emotional phenomena that are publicly inspectable, measurable and testable – a 'tough-minded, data-oriented approach to the tender-minded phenomena of human emotion.'[13] The idea of emotions as palpable states 'underlying' experimentally available data dissipates.[14] Thus perhaps 'Subjective experience must be dispensed with as a theoretical construct without objective utility.'[15] One fruit of this resolve has been the 'three-systems' approach to the study of emotion that has galvanised many researchers in psychology since the 1960s. What kind of headway does it make?

The 'systems' approach to emotion recognises the fact that emotion is not one-dimensional (certainly not just feeling, but not even just cognition or *just* anything else). Rather, there are several isolable dimensions in which emotions realise themselves, three in particular: evoked by situations, emotions take the form of verbal reports, physiological responses and overt behaviour. 'It is proposed that emotional behaviours are multiple system responses – verbal-cognitive, motor and physiological events that interact through interoceptive (neural and hormonal) and exteroceptive channels of communication.'[16] Some have been cautious about claiming that this is more than a heuristic device for guiding the scientific study of that about emotional phenomena which lends itself to scientific study: 'The three-system view is holding up very well as a study of emotion. It was, however, never intended as a full-blown theory of emotion.'[17]

However, it is not always easy to prevent methodological policy from becoming conceptual legislation, as this remark by a founder of the three-systems idea testifies: 'A coincidence of activity in more than one system is what we most confidently refer to as an emotion . . .'[18] It is a short step to the converse of this statement and the conclusion that emotions as the proprietary kinds of experience that people suppose themselves to have do not really occur – that folk-psychology reifies what are really loose associations of cognition, behaviour and physiology.

In fact, if the emotions were dissolved into arrays of these elements, it is not clear what could be salvaged of the distinctive identities people ascribe to them. For it seems that the level of correlation amongst cognition, behaviour, organic response and situation are actually quite low in emotional responses![19] Perhaps the most promising strategy on the part of the theory's proponents for preventing the break-up of an emotion such as fear into a weak pattern of events of independent kinds is to invoke the *function* of the emotion. The suggestion is that we should ask what, say, fear serves to do for its host, what it prepares him for. If it readies him to avoid what he perceives as a possible danger, then whatever specific acts, thoughts and physiological responses that so ready him comprise his fear; and in different situations different thoughts, acts and kinds of organic arousal may be needed to serve the same function, and hence realise fear.[20]

Plainly this requires of an emotion that there *be* something it is for. Let us call this the Function. Unfortunately, it is a cardinal error to assume that the Function is some proprietary kind of action, such as (in the case of fear) avoidance or communication. For what an emotion mobilises its host for is in part to satisfy the need which that emotion *itself* represents. Whatever my antecedent perceived need (for example, to avoid harm), whenever emotion is aroused a fresh urgency is born, a special urgency all of its own (that is, of the *fearsomeness* of the menacing harm). Most often, an emotion generates a need, which may be for catharsis (fear, curiosity, anger, depression), prolongation (delight), enhancement or repetition (thrill). Depending on the emotion, there may be a type of action (or reaction) that will satisfy its demand, for example, by danger avoidance (fear), aggression (anger), redemption (depression), continued contemplation of its object (delight), and so on. But the *proximate* Function of the action here is specifically to satisfy the emotional need. First and foremost, it is my delight in the dance that prompts me to repeat or continue it, not any end that my delight might serve, if such there be. The emotion plays an active part of its own in rousing its host to act and is not just a label for whatever states its host is in when roused to act. As we have seen, no rush of fear is necessary to prime a person for danger avoidance. *That* can happen coolly, even automatically. Fear cannot, therefore, be functionally defined as readiness to avoid danger or as whatever states of for example, the three systems that realise this readiness on the given occasion.

If an emotion were the underlying conditions that realise a state of incipient action, such an action would need to be in the offing, at least potentially (perhaps in imagination). The account just adumbrated, which sees the function of the action as in the first instance meeting a need created specifically by the advent of the emotional arousal, allows for a fact we have noticed before: there may be no action that could (directly) satisfy the emotive need. For retrospective emotions such as sorrow, guilt, grief, joy or relief, the time for action is past. In the first three cases, nothing now could undo what was done; in the second two cases, what needed doing has already been done.[21]

The question that must now have an answer is how an emotion creates its generic kind of need, for catharsis, removal, prolongation, repetition, enhancement and so on. The answer must be because of what it is like to its host, the tenor of its specific charge, in a word, its subjective quality. But there needn't be any such cast to cognitive, motor and physiological responses, and when there is, it, not its source in them, is what matters in explaining the emotion's immediate function. Such a cast is, however, inseparable from how the emotively affected person feels. This means that the subjectivity of feeling cannot after all be read out of our understanding of emotion.

– Notes –

1. Styron (1991), p. 16.
2. See Nagel (1979).
3. Ibid., p. 166.
4. Wilkes (1984), p. 240.
5. Dennett (1991), p. 447.
6. Wollheim (1992), p. 46.
7. Searle (1992), p. 95.
8. From Styron (1991), pp. 17 and 83, respectively.
9. Styron (1991), p. 68.
10. Fairbairn (1952), p. 5.
11. See Armstrong and Malcolm (1984), pp. 47 and 52, respectively.
12. Kramer (1993), p. 7.
13. Ohman and Birbaumer (1993), p. 14.
14. There is a certain temptation to think, conversely, of the experimentally available phenomena as underlying the experience of emotion!
15. Lang (1993), p. 19.
16. Ibid., p. 22.
17. Miller and Kozak (1993), p. 45.
18. Lang (1993), p. 23.
19. See ibid., pp. 11, 23–4. Note that the poor co-variation of events from the three systems in emotional reactions (and how *are* the latter then identified to start with?) is indeed cited as a reason against a 'unitary construct' view of emotions: 'We may note that the three-system view is more compatible with a dimensional than a categorical [sic] view of emotion ... this research may serve as an example that it is an essential ingredient of scientific psychology to break away from, and go beyond, the "folk psychology" inherent in the common language' (Ohman and Birbaumer (1993), p. 12).
20. See Miller and Kozac (1993), pp. 40–1.
21. What *need* is there in the latter two cases? Perhaps the need for it to be true that the wonderful thing has happened.

CHAPTER 7

Formulating Feelings

As I read it I experienced a strange icy joy of the weirdest kind.
Eric Lomax, The Railway Man

All the bitterness of life seemed to be served up to her on her plate;
and the steam rising from the boiled meat brought gusts of revulsion
from the depths of her soul.
Flaubert, Madame Bovary

– REPRESENTING FEELING: THE PROBLEM –

Like other subjective qualities, feelings can pass, or even linger, without
recognition. One can be in a certain state of feeling without thinking of
oneself as being in it or reflecting on what it is like. This, however, does
not make a feeling ineffable. An experiential quality that was just felt
can be recollected and can be susceptible to recognition. For this, no
propositional thought need have formed itself at the time (or at all in
the case of higher animals and pre-linguistic babies, who cannot be
supposed to lead affectless lives). Retrospectively, at least, the tenor of an
experience can often be cast in terms of a thought ('What a lot of fun it
was, come to think about it'/'I suppose really I was hating it all along').
May we conclude that the subjective complexion of feelings is at least
potentially propositional, that it is capable of precipitating itself into
thoughts of this form?[1]

There is room for limited optimism about this. We are not without
descriptive taxonomy for kinds of feeling. *Vexed, scared, disgusted, glad,
rueful, excited, dull, thrilled* are ways to feel; and there are many more of
these handy classificatory affective predicates. For all that, however, there
is no set menu of discrete feeling-kinds, no periodic table of the heart,
for our off-the-shelf categories to specify cleanly and without residue. In
their intensity and vivacity, feelings are seldom still; their qualities and
the shades of them are as various and unpredictable as the particular
situations and eventualities to which they are responses.

Now, where the nuances of a kind of experience can be finer-grained than is the classificatory scheme for them in the available language, the possibility of 'nuance ineffability' arises. That is, the niceties of the experience can't be put into words because there aren't the words for them in their full specificity:

> The limits of our schemas are the limits of our language, and *qua* perceivers we are so designed that the grain of conscious experience will inevitably be finer than that of our schemas, no matter how long, or how diligently, we practice.[2]

Is this true of emotional feeling? William Styron is not the only writer occupied with fidelity in the rendition of feeling to claim that it is.[3] Here is Flaubert:

> He had no perception – this man of such vast experience – of the dissimilarity of feeling that might underlie similarities of expression . . . Whereas the truth is that fullness of soul can sometimes overflow in utter vapidity of language, for none of us can ever express the exact measure of his needs or his thoughts or his sorrows; and human speech is like a cracked kettle on which we tap crude rhythms for bears to dance to, while we long to make music that will melt the stars.[4]

> Speech is a rolling machine that always stretches the feelings it expresses.[5]

A passage from Orwell's reflections on his service in the Spanish civil war points to a reason why the ready-made resources of language are apt to fall short:

> I have recorded some of the outward events, but I cannot record the feeling they left me with. It is all mixed up with sights, smells, and sounds that cannot be conveyed in writing: the smell of the trenches, the mountain dawns stretching away into inconceivable distances, the frosty crackle of bullets, the roar and glare of bombs; the clear cold light of the Barcelona mornings, and the stamp of boots in the barrack yard, back in December when people still believed in the revolution; and the food-queues and the red and black flags and the faces of the Spanish militiamen; above all the faces of militiamen . . .[6]

The way it felt is shown here to depend on an elaborate conjunction and admixture of things experienced at a certain time by a particular individual.

How, and how successfully, then, can we represent feelings? We will see that the resources that language has for characterising affect are not actually confined to coarse-grained, generalising taxonomic vocabulary. The limit possibilities seem to be, on the one hand, that the nuances of feeling may be inexpressible, or, on the other hand, that they actually have retrievable propositional content.[7] Must we land at either of these poles?

– FEELING AND PRIVACY –

How a feeling feels is what makes it the feeling it is. This is so natural a claim as to seem a truism. But what a slippery truism it turns out to be. For it at least sounds like a claim that the character of a feeling comes down to phenomenal properties that are registered introspectively, as if outwardly invisible colours were being inwardly viewed. Such properties would, of course, need to be susceptible to identification and delineation. Yet someone could be subject to a state with such properties without their being disclosed or expressively evinced; for they are not actually properties of the kinds of utterance, the demeanour, or comportment that may be treated as expressive of them and as their outward criteria (or of the thoughts charged with them).[8] Does this make them epistemologically private? The assumption that subjectivity means privacy of the sort attacked by Wittgenstein was one of Wilkes' reasons for rejecting subjectivity, and she will not be alone in this.

It is important to realise, therefore, that this problem does not really arise. A mind that was an array of states of the sort which Wittgenstein's private diarist strives to catalogue would consist exclusively rather than intermittently of states that were like something only to those who were in them. These states, in turn, would have to consist in what they were like to the respective individuals and in nothing else.[9] They could be unlike anything anyone else ever underwent (if there was anyone else).

What is fatal to *this* idea is that it would make the mind ineffable in its entirety, thus altogether disabling the capacity for introspection which was supposed to be its workhorse. For the only purchase language could get on items that were undisclosable (and so effectively incommensurable as between minds) would be by acts of unrelievedly solitary ostension that were uncheckable except by further acts of inner ostension.[10] This would not permit word usage to establish itself on a genuinely rule-governed basis.[11]

Now, the claim that emotional feelings have subjective qualities neither makes the claims nor faces the difficulties envisaged by Wittgenstein and other critics of traditional dualism. The claim is not that feelings consist in nothing but their phenomenal properties, or that such properties can bear no intelligible relationships to the public world which might serve to identify them, or that they are always unique in kind to each individual having them. Nor is there any implication that the mind generally (thoughts, desires, intentions and so on) could comprise only such items.

To assert that how a feeling feels is an aspect it has only to a person feeling it, does not entail that the subjective character of a feeling can't be similar from person to person or that it is incommunicable.

What, then, *does* give me purchase on what I am feeling? To answer this, we must ask how the character of my feeling is related to the wider world? There are several answers to this question. Two of them were prefigured in the general discussion of the idea of subjectivity. As a particular type of animal, I share a constitution with others of my kind; and as a social animal, they and I inhabit a common social world (at least culture by culture). In these two ways, I do not stand to other people as we would stand to a lion who could talk or as one Wittgensteinian private diarist would stand to another.

This common background, together with the resources of language and imagination which it renders possible, make individual differences largely scrutable. Even the refined peculiarities that may indeed distinguish one person's feelings from anyone else's become *approximately* locatable (at least in the sane) – sufficiently to prevent total incomprehension. Everyone knows well enough what feeling depressed is like to ensure that William Styron is no Private Diarist when he writes of 'feeling in my mind a sensation close to, but indescribably different from, actual pain'[12] – although only an unfortunate minority are fully privy to what Styron's words gesture at. The conditions of reference of the word 'depressed' are a moving feast, neither perfectly public nor inaccessibly private. *Mutatis mutandis* for other affective states.[13] Public meaning does not preclude private reference. Private reference (a degree of it) would preclude public sense only where it constituted the whole of a word's meaning. And words for feelings are never so semantically impoverished as that.

These rather general considerations are a start in understanding how a public language can give purchase on subjective qualities of experience without dissolving them. A closer look at how feelings are actually depicted and communicated will consolidate this and complete the argument developed earlier that feelings, and therefore the emotions they may instantiate, are not composed just of the emotive thoughts distinctive of them.

– Ties with the Public World –

A point of view that is no one else's, however absorbing it may be, can still be a point of view on something other than itself (as are, for example, wistfulness or anxiousness). And what it is like to its host can show itself in the descriptions of things that it makes natural. Just how do descriptions of the world figure in the representation of feelings? How does the identification of a feeling depend on its circumstances?

Your slighting remark cut me to the quick. Here *cause* (your harsh remark) identifies. However, it is not always the cause that identifies. I may not actually realise what hurt me (or what it was about your remark) until later, if at all. Yet I may realise full well from the start what it is I feel (hurt) and puzzle over why. It is possible to wake up in an irritated frame of mind without an inkling as to why.

How can I realise what I feel (however inchoate: edgy, irritable) when I don't realise why? What a feeling feels like can present itself in a range of ways that are independent both of direct reference to phenomenological qualities and to causes. What tells me how I feel may be what I feel *like*, in the sense of how I feel myself disposed to respond in the moment. Such a disposition can be either transitive or intransitive. That is, it may be a desire, something I feel like doing then or it may be an intimation of what I am about to do, something that is about to happen in me. In the first vein, I may feel like slapping someone in the face, jumping up and down (for joy), calling a halt, gathering someone up in my arms. In the second, I may feel on the verge of crying, or my gorge rising, my temper fraying, my nerve failing, or myself about to scream.

Obviously, bodily sensations may loom large in intransitive 'feeling like'; and anyway they are themselves a third way in which emotional feelings display themselves. Thus, shock may (but need not) come as a visceral jolt. Foreboding may gnaw away at me in the pit of my stomach; leadenness of limb and voice may signal despair; the body of someone who is excited may course with energy; people blush with embarrassment and are wide-eyed with astonishment. These physical responses are more than incidental effects of the respective emotional feelings.

In fact, ever since the James–Lange theory was proposed, there has been a standing temptation to view emotional feelings as bodily feelings. This can be encouraged by the belief that emotional feelings taken in themselves are too often just amorphous excitations,[14] and that the same holds of states of bodily feeling. It may be held that the physical agitations experienced in the course of an emotion – joy and sorrow, for instance, or fear and triumph – are not obviously distinguishable.[15] So perhaps the emotional *feelings* just are the non-self-distinguishing states of physical arousal marked off as episodes of emotion only by their causes, by the circumstances in which they occur and by our attitudes to them in these circumstances.[16]

Even if emotional feelings, such as joy and sorrow, lend themselves being distinguished and identified in these ways, they can still differ in how they feel. For the feeling of joy and of sorrow is not confined to the visceral arousal it may involve, nor need it involve such arousal at all. The pain of sorrow, the sunken feeling of dejection and the brightness of elation are palpably unalike. And unlike swollen tear ducts and churning viscera, they are not just feelings of overt bodily states. Despite the extensive overlap of visceral and emotional feeling, feeling does not always come down to bodily feeling. Some bodily feelings, such as sensations of nausea or dizziness, are not emotional at all; on the other hand, emotive feeling may not carry any bodily charge with it – many vivid emotional feelings are not conspicuously visceral (desolation, wistfulness). And when emotional feeling does occur in company with physical arousal, the two may still be distinct. Thus, how we like having a given bodily feeling may itself be a matter of feeling, and how we feel about a bodily feeling or about having it (anxious, delighted, disappointed) is not that bodily feeling. Nor is this feeling the context of the bodily feeling, though it may depend on that context. For instance, physical strain may feel debilitating (when humping luggage) or exhilarating (a runner's final heat); a touch may be soothing (from a loved one) or (from a molester) loathsome. Some quite distinctive states of feeling may not involve physical feelings or be tied to any definite context or ground: Moods. Notice also that some physical sensations that can be cited to characterise feelings of an emotion can characterise them only figuratively: 'nauseated', 'dizzy', 'stung', 'uplifted', 'hot', 'tickled'. So used, these terms need not refer to the actual physical sensations they mention.

Feelings that are *feelings like* encompass more than bodily feelings. To feel like coming over and shaking your hand or like succumbing to an outburst need not be to feel any particular sensation. However, not even these broader *feelings like* suffice to characterise every type of emotive feeling.[17] For some feelings, there may not be anything I directly feel like doing. Relief, grief and guilt, for example, respond to consummated actions rather than anticipate or substitute for them; they are not transitive feelings like. They may be intransitive: I feel like I can breathe freely again (relief) or like crying (grief); but they don't have to take just these forms. And desolation or serenity seem hard to identify with anything I am (directly) disposed to do. Besides, when we try to flesh out our feelings, the things we say we feel we are about to do, or feel like doing, are often literal impossibilities. We should not be misled by expressions such as 'I could just scream!', which serves notice that the way I feel is the way one feels when one needs to scream. For very many of the things we claim to feel like have the form of 'I could just explode!', 'I could tear you limb from limb', 'My heart melted', 'I felt my blood curdle', or 'I felt a stab of remorse'. How I feel when I say I feel like I'm going to explode is, of course, not at all how I would actually feel if I were literally about to explode; nor is literally exploding what I mean to say I feel like doing when I say it is. The characterisation of feeling in terms of *feeling like* (both transitive and intransitive) is divided as between the literal and the figurative. The only thing of which the description is true can be how I feel. As a description of objective circumstances it may not even make sense ('burst with joy'). It can have sense only to someone who can feel or imagine feeling as I say I feel.

The same goes for *as if*, even though its compass is wider still than *feels like* ('I felt as if something pervasive and ominous lurked behind the innocuous frontage of everyday life'). *As if* allows us to draw descriptively on a wider range of phenomena than our own dispositions to react (lashing out, crying), which transitive and intransitive 'feeling like' descriptions invoke. A description of feeling can draw upon circumstances in the public world using the expression 'as if' to preserve the connection with the paradigmatic circumstances of its occurrence even when these are not actually believed to be (or construed as) present. Hence, the fact that feelings of an emotion can become detached from the judgements that typify that emotion-type does not prevent them from being *character-ised* by means of propositions or mean they must be known solely by introspection.

Yet, *as if* shares the ambiguity noted above between the literal and the figurative. Often a feeling may be identified by likening it to feelings that arise in the paradigmatic circumstances that make sense of it ('The rebuke was sudden: it was as if I had been slapped across the face'). But not only can we identify a feeling by a reference to paradigmatic circumstances that occasion or warrant feelings of its kind, we can also capture it by 'as if' descriptions that are analogical or metaphorical. Here feelings are delineated by invoking images of things that are perfectly public but which never *actually* occasion feelings of the kind they are being used to depict and sometimes never could. Feeling 'over the moon' isn't necessarily how someone who really was over the moon would feel; and someone can feel 'as if a mountain had fallen on him' even though if it had, he would feel nothing. We are not saying we feel as we would if these circumstances were realised or that we feel as if they were realised.

– CAPTURING FEELING: METAPHOR –

Feeling is caught best of all in figurative language. Hope dawns, glimmers and fades; it can rise up and roll back a suffocating fog of gloom. In such descriptions, the literal circumstances and properties appealed to actually form no part of the truth-conditions of the description. Their sense, whether they are apt and how, is apparent only from the vantagepoint of a person to whose feeling they are made to refer (or to others capable of occupying such a vantagepoint or of imagining it).

Metaphor, in particular, lends an oblique public character to feelings. By means of it they may be captured and communicated without being directly referred to or described at all. Love is evoked by speaking of a rose; the beloved is rendered as a summer's day, in terms that convey the feeling towards her. There is even a certain abstraction here from a feeling's status as an inward event in someone's personal history. The focus is more on what it is like than on whose it is. Metaphors for feelings contrive to be expressive without being confessional. Metaphors can give voice to feelings without trying to describe them as private objects. For, the *objects* alluded to are neither undisclosable nor situated in some private space. They can embody the subjective complexion of a feeling whilst remaining impersonal.

Is there something a metaphor serves to say, a definite propositional content which it in effect affirms or entertains? – If so, that might be seen as a thought constitutive of the feeling. The natural word for what a metaphor of feeling does is *evocation*. Of course someone who develops a metaphor for a feeling has the belief that this metaphor fits that feeling. But is the metaphor itself a belief, either about the feeling or perhaps about what the feeling is about (or an unaffirmed thought of either of these)? For this to be so, there would have to be a proposition the person was expressing in using the metaphor other than that this metaphor was apt. But if there is something we are trying to say by means of the metaphor that it does not already show, or if we can state what it does show, why use it in the first place?

Admittedly, some metaphors do seem thus dispensable. (Perhaps 'granite-jawed' just comes down to 'tense with resolution'). Where this is so, to believe something to be a good metaphor would be to believe these propositions or portray something in terms of them. So if the whole power of metaphor lay in descriptive ripeness of this sort, metaphors would indeed come down to nascent, inchoate thoughts or to devices for suggesting these.[18]

Many philosophers have assumed that, *au fond*, this is the case. The presumption is that metaphors serve to convey a thought with propositional content that can be assessed for truth or falsity, that this is their primary function rather than one of their incidental, if useful, effects (as when the image of a snake holding the tip of its own tail in its mouth prompted Kekule to conclude that the atomic chain of the benzine molecule forms a circle). After all, metaphors are made out of words. Even though its metaphorical use may not be a word's standard use, it is natural to think that its force as a metaphor somehow depends on its meaning. The words in a metaphorical utterance seem to be used to say something, and what they are being used to say may be presumed to be informational, a matter of propositional content.

At its simplest, the thesis is that one way or another, by getting us to consider one thing in terms of something else, typically quite unlike it, a metaphor asserts (indicates) a comparison: 'a good metaphor implies an intuitive perception of similarity in dissimilars'.[19] A predicate is supposed to carry over unexpectedly from one context to another.[20]

Given that the delineation of feeling is particularly reliant on metaphor, feelings would resolve into articulable thoughts if metaphors did serve primarily to propose propositional descriptions. Yet this general conception of metaphor is open to challenge. Its leading opponent, Donald Davidson, rejects the idea that 'associated with a metaphor is a cognitive content that its author wishes to convey and that the interpreter must grasp if he is to get the message'.[21] The Burden of a metaphor need be 'neither finite in scope nor propositional in character'.[22] In trying to understand the depiction of feeling, our concern is similarly negative. It is not with how metaphors do work so much as whether they work via propositional content. In particular, do they rely on isolating certain predicates of the thing used as a metaphor and asserting them of the subject of that metaphor (or representing it through them)?[23]

What is wrong with the idea that metaphorical meaning rests on propositional content? A principal difficulty is that it does not always seem possible to find another predicate to characterise a thing that presents what a metaphor presents. There is more than one reason for this. At the very least, it can be remarkably difficult to specify just which is the key property. A borderline case would be: 'when she is contradicted, her gracious smile hardens to granite, and her eyes become icepicks'.[24] We at once recognise these qualities of expression, yet the actual facial changes that make for these alterations of countenance are not thereby identified and remain quite elusive. 'The smile sets' takes us some way with 'hardens to granite' but what makes for eyes like icepicks resists easy identification (in due course, we will notice yet harder cases). This difficulty is compounded by the fecundity of metaphors. A good metaphor may be rich in that the more we consider it, the more ways it turns out to apply. It may admit of development over time in multiple and unpredictable ways, and it isn't clear where, if anywhere, the limits to its depictive potential are. Perhaps the list is not too long for 'iron willed', but how about 'iron in the soul'?

There may also be novelty in the way in which a metaphor presents its subject. It need not rely on antecedently identifiable properties of the subject: 'new analogies might come to light which the originator of the metaphor had never envisaged, so could not have been part of that person's meaning-intention'.[25] 'She has a mouth like a bag with the drawstring pulled tight' might jolt one into noticing this feature for the first time, that is, enlarge rather than reiterate one's perception of how she looks.

Wherever these two things are true, the prospects of specifying *which* proposition a metaphor means, or which one the speaker means to assert, are dim.

Even if we did specify the proposition, that might not get us anywhere. In the example above, when her eyes become icepicks (as metaphors go, lively but not very extended and only moderately deep) they do *point at* just as an icepick can (that is, in a direction in space), but they are not *pointed* (or *sharp, narrow, hard, cold* and *deadly*) in the same way an icepick is, though they precisely are all these things metaphorically. A predicate does not project unmodified from a non-metaphorical into a metaphorical context. Iron cannot, *except metaphorically*, be stubborn, persistent or headstrong.[26]

It can be argued that the same property is instantiated in both contexts at a sufficient level of abstraction (an 'iron' will, like an iron bar, is 'difficult to change once set').[27] Yet metaphors seem quite the opposite of abstract; anyway, abstracted properties like *rigid* or *difficult to change* (taken literally) altogether fail to present what the metaphor presents. Even if you could name the property, you would miss the point of the metaphor for it. The failure here owes, I think, to this: what matters is not which property is being gotten at but the *way* this subject has that property, what *its* having that property is like. Thus, even if there always were a single property of sufficient abstraction that a term marked in both its non-metaphorical uses and its metaphorical uses, it cannot realise itself in the same form across these contexts. The force of the metaphor is evidently not captured by reciting what the property is in its abstract, transferable form (the advantage of calling a right-wing movement the 'Iron Guard' instead of 'The-Difficult-to-Change-Once-Set Guard' is more than one of brevity). In fact, the literal properties are not characterised at all. Without plumbing the literal properties underlying the change to icepick eyes, the metaphor does depict that alteration; and it depicts it in terms of its effect on beholders, the impression it makes.[28] Were one in turn to enlarge on that impression in a way that really conveyed it ('a look that willed her interlocutor out of existence on the spot'), further resort to metaphor would be needed.

So, the understanding of a metaphor can itself involve metaphors. Where it does, the picture of metaphor as merely foreshadowing a proper grasp of its subject is less secure. If there are subjects which scarcely admit of literal description and yet are richly susceptible to metaphorical characterisation, the reductivist view of metaphor seems little better than an endlessly updated blank cheque.[29] And it does often appear that a metaphor and its unfolding possess a subtlety that there is no way of capturing short of further metaphor. (Could Shakespeare have completed the comparison of his beloved to a summer's day with straightforward descriptions? If so, why didn't he? And if he couldn't, who could?)

Our inability to say in other terms what a metaphor is trying to say (or show) will be at its height wherever the rule-governed vocabulary of literal description is minimal. Such a medium must be explored with the aid of imported resources. Three areas that exemplify this are tastes, feelings and music (there are others). They are areas in which it is not just that paraphrases of metaphorical language are less exciting or are hard to come by but rather that paraphrase is scarcely possible. Consider the case of wine-and whisky-tasting, where (literal) terms such as 'sweet', 'sour', 'bitter' quickly give way to terms such as 'fragrant', 'fruity', 'sharp', 'smooth' and from there to further semantic pastures: 'An explosive start and a steep, bright finish with a touch of mellowness about it and a rich afterglow. Memorable.' In such a description even a word like 'smooth' (for example, in the phrase, 'a smooth finish') needn't any longer be referring to the actual felt mechanical texture of the liquid (as 'viscous' or 'thin' do). Usage and semantic rules do not establish what this phrase means as applied to the characteristic taste of a brand of whisky. When I receive a postcard from an exotic place, I can gather what is being described from the words alone. But not here. Here I cannot understand the description from the words alone. The Taster's report is a closed book to a teetotaller; not to have tasted is not to understand. Experience is needed to show a reader the tastes a discriminating taster discriminates. The words then show the taste in a certain light; and the taste shows the words' sense.

A metaphorical description may also differ from a literal one (or from a metaphorical description that can be replaced by a literal one) in not being true or false of that for which it is apt or inapt. Metaphors in these contexts, then, are not really beliefs or expressions of beliefs.[30] Thus, it is not clear that diverse metaphors for the same thing *contradict* one another. The same state or event might admit of contrasting metaphorical characterisations without one being true and the others false, or one being the right one. A conflict of metaphors would more resemble holding up two contrasting portraits of a face to that face than falsifying a proposition.

It may be that emotional feelings are more susceptible to construction by metaphor than sensations are. Though more ephemeral than emotions, feelings can be less ephemeral than sensations such as tastes. Feelings, such as anxiety or high spirits, can linger and outlast the fading of their grounds or, like anticipation and dread, be summoned and sustained by the mere thought of their causes, as sensations, with their close dependence on precise physical causes, cannot. Consequently, the metaphorical casting of a feeling has more of a chance of acting on the feeling and transfiguring it, shaping rather than just recording. Feelings can be completed in metaphor. Poetry, or at least the poetic use of language, can be more than a spectator in the emotional life. (It is for this reason that the best term for their relation to their subject-matter is *evocation*, with its double sense, at once depictive and active.)

This is not to say, however, that what a feeling is like without benefit of metaphorical christening plays no part in the application of metaphor to it. If metaphorical description is not a judgement and does not aspire quite to truth, it still needs to be *apt* (success and failure are possible in this). To invent too freely would be fictionalise feeling, a fairyland that it is only too possible to enter. Metaphor-making needn't be free image-spinning. A feeling allows images that do not distort it to be discriminated from those that do. It can be clear that some metaphors are better than others, even if no full account can be given of why. The analogy here is with aspectual seeing and its *limits*. How I see an aspectual ambiguous figure (for example, the Necker cube as three-dimensional and solid) is a function of more than what I see. Yet what I see (the lines conjoined just so) constrains how I can see the figure: I can't see the Necker figure as a duck or a rabbit or the duck–rabbit figure as a cube.

– Evocation: Beyond Propositions –

The deflationary view of metaphor is that either it is a place-holder for some literal statement – a way of saying something we don't yet quite know how to say directly (for example, the 'pull' of gravity or 'superstrings' in cosmology). It was argued above, however, that this is not so where the only or most suitable language is metaphorical, as in the depiction of feelings.[31] How well is this claim borne out in practice? In the Song of Solomon we read,

> Because of the savour of thy good ointments
> thy name is as ointment poured forth . . .
> A bundle of myrrh is my well-beloved unto me;
> he shall lie all night betwixt my breasts.
> Behold, thou art fair, my beloved, yea,
> pleasant: also our bed is green.
> The beams of our house are cedar, and our
> rafters of fir.[32]

Apparently, a lover is being rejoiced in. Clearly, to seek for a fact about the lover or their life together which these lines rejoice *that* would not tap a propositional core ('It's wonderful to be with you'), but would altogether miss the burden of sentiment in these lines. Even in simpler cases where there is a propositional burden to the metaphor ('honour bright' is honour that always prevails), the metaphor does not just consist in the suggestion of this proposition, nor is that its primary interest. It is clear from the Song of Solomon passage that what it is the primary function of the metaphors to indicate is *how* the presence of the beloved is wonderful.

Notice that as the word 'evoke' suggests, the nature of a feeling may be conveyed in two ways: by being characterised or by being aroused. This distinction is pertinent to the expression of feeling in music. Music is the clearest instance in which showing a feeling is not a matter of saying (or hence of believing) anything about it. In at least some cases it is not clear that what a feeling feels like (and therefore is) *can* be fully captured by language, however vivid and dextrous. This is where the expressive power of music comes into its own. We need not detain ourselves over how music manages to express feeling or whether that is the primary function of music. Whatever may be said about these matters, it is clear that music can do this and do it with a fidelity that words labour to match. Try to put into words the sentiment evoked (and readily identified without any verbal clues) by the Nimrod theme in Elgar's *Enigma Variations*. However well you do it, your efforts are unlikely to be an adequate substitute for hearing the theme.

– FEELING AS EXCEEDING THOUGHT –

What now of our original question about feeling and representation? Must there be a propositional core to a feeling that can be teased out of it? Or can many feelings and their textures be inexpressible? And are these alternatives exclusive?

Sometimes the quality of a feeling can be rendered in terms of the person's conceptualisations, as in a gloomy outlook or manic expectations. But we have seen that a plausible informing *conceptualisation* may be hard to come by or fall short, as in disgust, panic, hate, rage, misery and many thrills and excitements. And notice that even where a satisfactory description is available, it is a fallacy to identify what is felt with this description. The description may be generated only later. It may never be generated. Or no available description may seem adequate – there may be no re-creating a trauma or the captivating charm of a moment. Besides, we have seen that telling portrayals of all but the simplest feelings, where they are possible, veer into metaphor, and a good metaphor does not serve to propose a proposition, a specifiable animating thought.

If feelings cannot be relied on to incorporate thoughts and cannot be 'linguified', are we driven to the opposite pole? – Can they be ineffable? Well, it is as much a fallacy to infer from the absence of a governing thought at the heart of a feeling that there can be no description of it, as it is to treat such a description as the content of the feeling. But I will slightly fudge the question of ineffability and just note how specific, non-abstracting and subtle the resources of metaphor are and how the writers we have heard complain the loudest about ineffability are among the best at depicting refinements of feeling. At least we can confront the subjectivity of experience here without being driven either into the philosophical *cul de sac* of a pure phenomenology or into that of silence. And that's a lot.

– CONSEQUENCES FOR THE PHILOSOPHY OF EMOTION –

Almost every theory of emotion we have considered so far is partly true. This is not to say that any of them are part of the truth. There may be no omnibus answer to the question 'What is an emotion?' waiting to be discovered. It needn't be a well-formed question. Attempts to set out an answer to it tend to be as interesting for their failings as for their strengths. Emotions (even of the same type) vary considerably in what they may involve, and in what is salient in them while they last and from instance to instance. The more general we try to be about emotions, the more disjunctive our account must become. Perhaps most of the interesting questions about the emotions are of the more particular kind. But it will not avail to approach such questions hobbled by doctrinal do's and don'ts. Above all, the temptation to ignore emotional feeling or to force it into some propositional form must be resisted.

That means allowing for the possibility in some cases of emotion (and perhaps even in many) of a minimal role for thought, be it belief or non-assertional imagining. Of course, a minimal role is still a role. For, even where what I think is not the whole of what I feel, it gives at least a partially determinate reference or intentionality to my emotions (in this respect, for example, anxiety that something unspecified may be going badly wrong is an advance on anxiety that is merely an undirected state of mind). The representation of feeling does not exhaust the characterisation of emotion. If affect does not reduce to thought in the composition of an emotion, neither does it replace thought. The stress on the role of the one at the expense of the other that informs debates about the nature of emotion only points to their respective contributions, to their relations.

And what are these? Typically, emotions incorporate both thought, ranging from imaginings to judgements, *and* feelings (at least dispositionally). Many properties of emotions (including, as we shall see, their soundness) depend on the distinctness of these elements and on their precise relations. What is usually a mistake, however, is to treat emotions as mere associations or clusters of these elements. Often the relation is one exhibited in this example (from *Nostromo*) of an old man realising that his wife has died,

> The thought that no call from him would ever again evoke the answer of her voice made him drop heavily into the chair with a loud groan, wrung out by the pain as of a keen blade piercing his breast.[33]

Here the acknowledged circumstances fix the general type of emotion undergone (grief), whilst its precise nature is completed in the feeling the man experiences. How he feels is portrayed in terms that do not just replicate the propositional content of his acknowledgement (judgement) and need not describe any thought he has. He needn't reflect that this is how he feels for it to be how he feels, though he must recognise (believe) that his wife's voice will no longer answer him if he is to suffer this particular felt twist of grief.

In cases of this sort, the person's outright judgement determines the general type of the emotion without constituting the specific form in which it is realised as affect. Hence the belief can serve both to identify the emotion and to cause it, yet without constituting it. This obviates the logical problem with the idea that emotions should at once comprise cognitions and be caused by them (raised in Chapter 1).

It would be wrong, however, to elevate the idea that judgements fix the type-identity and feelings determine the refinements into a paradigm. In the quote from *The Railway Man* at the head of this chapter, an ex-POW realises that the letter in his hand requesting contact is from his Japanese tormentor of decades ago and reads it as an appeal made in repentance. Now, the belief and the construal here do not yet fix the emotion-*type* of the reaction that overtakes him as he reads. There may be no pre-defined category for what gathers in him. His judgements and perceptions only prime him for a response that resolves itself largely in the form of feelings, which he may only retrospectively have formulated as 'an icy joy of the weirdest kind'.

Emotions can also bring certain complications to people's lives which can only be understood for what they are once emotional feeling is recognised as a distinct, and distinctive, phenomenon that has a life of its own and brings qualities to experience that it would otherwise lack, for better and for worse. Of the complications that trade on the autonomy of feeling, irrationality is only one, and it does not deserve to be the most notorious. There is another way in which feeling is more unequivocally, and more subtly, subversive of the emotions. To that we are now in a position to turn.

– NOTES –

1. 'of this form' is meant to leave open the question whether thoughts can include feeling-laden images whose expression needs no verbal interpretation – for instance, sights or sounds that are immediately felt as poignant, bleak, sublime, disgusting,

horrifying and so on, which offer less joy to cognitive treatment than do formulable feelings.

2. Raffman (1993), p. 136. She defends this thesis with respect to our reception of music against Dennett's general claim that, as she puts it, 'if I really put my mind to it, I could report exhaustively the contents of conscious awareness' (p. 131). She thinks ineffability extends to 'the many determinate shades and shapes and tastes and textures of everyday life' (p. 96). There seems no reason to deny it to the shades and textures of emotive feelings.

3. In the case of the melancholia in depression, Styron notes that many psychiatrists 'simply do not seem to be able to comprehend the nature and depth of the anguish their patients are undergoing' (1991; p. 68). Not surprisingly, for 'since antiquity . . . chroniclers of the human spirit have been wrestling with a vocabulary that might give proper expression to the desolation of melancholia' (ibid., pp. 82–3).

4. Flaubert (1971), pp. 215–16.

5. Ibid., p. 267.

6. Orwell (1978), p. 219.

7. Recall that the hedonic-cognitive approach to feeling needs to differentiate feelings via distinctions in the contents of pleasurable/painful thoughts they are said to involve, a view that would seem to turn on the truth of the second alternative.

8. This was argued in Chapter 6.

9. 'Suppose I didn't have any natural expression for the sensation, but only had the sensation. And now I simply *associate* names with sensations and use these names in descriptions' Wittgenstein (1953), p. 256.

   'The individual words of this language are to refer to what can only be known to the person speaking; to his immediate private sensations. So another person cannot understand the language' (ibid., p. 243).

10. 'Well, that is done precisely by the concentration of my attention; for in this way I impress on myself the connection between the sign and the sensation. But "I impress it on myself" can only mean: this process brings it about that I remember the connection *right* in the future. But in the present case I have no criterion of correctness. One would like to say: whatever is going to seem right to me is right. And that only means that here one can't talk about "right"' (ibid., p. 258).

11. 'The word "agreement" and the word "rule" are *related* to one another, they are cousins. If I teach anyone the use of the one word, he learns the use of the other with it' (ibid., p. 224).

12. Styron (1991), p. 16.

13. Thus, ineffability of an experience (a) may be possible, (b) can only be partial, (c) needn't be an unsharable or even unique experience of a single individual. As to (b): even appropriate language for a feeling can fail to convey it, as the passage from *Madame Bovary* quoted on p. 91 suggests. Sometimes, the resistance to description is more complete. Styron continues the passage quoted in note 12 above as follows:

    this leads me to touch again on the elusive nature of such distress. That the word 'indescribable' should present itself is not fortuitous, since it has to be emphasised that if the pain were readily describable most of the countless sufferers from this ancient affliction would have been able to confidently depict for their friends and loved ones (even their physicians) some of the actual dimensions of their torment, and perhaps elicit a comprehension that has been generally lacking; such incomprehension has usually been due not to a failure of sympathy but to the basic inability of healthy people to imagine a form of torment so alien to everyday experience . . . hence the frustrated sense of inadequacy found in the work of even the greatest artists [who have undergone and tried to convey this dysphoria].

(Styron (1991), pp. 16–17)

14. Consider, once again, Bedford's (1956) examples of indignation and annoyance and of shame and embarrassment (pp. 111 and 116, respectively); also the claim cited by Bedford that 'there is little evidence that a peculiar, unique type of consciousness accompanies and identifies the different emotions' (ibid., p. 100).
15. Lyons (1980), pp. 133–5.
16. See, for instance, ibid., ch. 8. Obviously, the Singer–Schacter experiment would lend credence to this approach; however, see Reisenzein (1983).
17. This treatment of emotional feeling would be the natural partner of the attempts to understand emotions via their relation to dispositions to act, that is, as 'magical' substitutes for actions or as the residual perturbations of inhibited actions, or as states of preparedness to act, which are envisaged, respectively by Hampshire (1976), Sartre (1962) and Lang (1993).
18. As Blackburn maintains (1984), p. 16.
19. Aristotle, *Poetics*, 1459a.
20. Defenders of this general approach differ as to just how this feat of predication works. Beardsley, for instance, thinks there is a difference between the properties a term denotes, which give it its sense, and its connotations, beliefs about the sense-determining properties, which Beardsley calls 'credence properties'. The metaphorical use of a term involves replacing the elements of the term's sense by some of the beliefs merely associated with it. This results in a change of sense in the term when it is used metaphorically – Beardsley (1978). By contrast, for Cohen (1972 and 1979), all properties recognised to pertain to a term are semantic features of it and the term becomes metaphorical by selectively cancelling out various of its semantic features (presumably, in 'iron will' *ferrous* drops out of 'iron'). So the sense of a metaphorical term is already there in the literal context and does not itself change in the transition.
21. Davidson (1984).
22. Ibid. The suspicion that the message of metaphors is not specifically propositional was John Locke's reason why they were 'wholly to be avoided'. Writers who share Locke's doubts but not his strictures include Cooper (1986) and Rorty (1987).
23. The most searching case for a negative answer to this question is found in David Cooper (1986), chs 2 and 4.
24. James Wolcott on Adrianna Stanissopolis-Huffington, 'Beyond the Values of Supervixens', *New Yorker*, 13 February 1995, p. 91.
25. Lamarque (1994), p. 362.
26. See ibid., p. 358.
27. As Beardsley claims (1978), p. 13.
28. Certainly, there are cognitive messages here too. Part of the metaphor's potency rests on the brittle and aggressive dispositions it suggests that are shadowed in her sudden reaction to contradiction. But asserting these as psychological facts about her clearly does not exhaust the work of the metaphor.
29. This is one sense in which metaphor 'involves the *exploration* rather than the *translation* of meaning' (Lamarque (1994), p. 365).
30. The question as to what metaphors do may hang less on what metaphor is than on its subject-matter.
31. It might seem that this account of metaphor coincides with the notion of construal discussed in earlier chapters. Thus, neither a metaphorical description of something as x nor a construal of something as y amount to a belief that the respective things are x or y. In a construal, however, I think of the thing as though it were y (but

without supposing this). I construe you as hostile, as if it were true that you were an enemy, even though I don't actually claim that you are; it is a moment of paranoia which I recognise for what it is. This is real territory, admittedly, but not that of metaphor. Not only is Shakespeare in Sonnet XVIII not asserting that his beloved is like a summer's day as one summer's day is like another, he is also not suggesting that it is as if she were, which makes no sense at all.

32. Song of Solomon I: 2,13,16,17.
33. Conrad (1994), p. 384.

CHAPTER 8

Feeling and the Corruption of Emotion

Whosoever will save his life shall lose it.

Matthew, 16: 25

The previous chapters have exerted themselves to isolate and dramatise the role of feeling in emotions. The search has been for the differences between the quality of affective arousal that may animate an emotional state and the cognitive attitudes that make for the emotion, even where these attitudes are subassertional. This has extended to the recognition that emotive feeling need not be esoteric or inexpressible. The way a person feels may actually form the leading edge of the thought he develops about the situation rather than the other way around. The subjective complexion of feeling defines the emotion and world alike.

However, we may exalt in this potential for affective autonomy only up to a point. Beliefs still form the conceptual conditions of many emotions (*pride* still requires approval and some form of identification, for instance). But belief can have a further, more elusive sustaining role in emotions. It can give what we might call *authenticity* to emotions where feelings of these emotions signally cannot. It would be well to bring our treatment of the emotions full circle by eliciting this distinct and morally sensitive part played by belief in the emotional life.

– An Affective Pathology –

Emotions can be passions, but need passions be emotions? We easily assume that feelings of the kind typical of a given emotion amount to that emotion. ('I know what I feel' is commonly rated a touchstone for the workaday epistemology of emotion.) I will suggest that it is not, in any sense of the word, safe to presume this. It is worth exploring the pitfalls of this misconception, which so readily bedevils the life of the emotions and which is so difficult to resist. Understanding it may facilitate resistance.

Below is a passage from George Orwell's *Coming Up for Air*. What follows it is an attempt to understand the sort of phenomenon Orwell evokes, which is still very much with us, if not always in such a lurid form. The setting of this passage is a political lecture in a London pub just prior to the Second World War.

Do you ever go to lectures, public meetings, and whatnot? At the beginning I wasn't exactly listening. The lecturer was a rather mean-looking little chap, but a good speaker. White face, very mobile mouth, and the rather grating voice that they get from constant speaking. Of course he was pitching into Hitler and the Nazis. I wasn't particularly keen to hear what he was saying – get the same stuff in the *News Chronicle* every morning – but his voice came across to me as a kind of burr-burr-burr, with now and again a phrase that stuck out and caught my attention. 'Bestial atrocities . . . Hideous outbursts of sadism . . . Rubber truncheons . . . fascism . . . Defence of democracy . . . Democracy . . . Fascism . . . Democracy . . . Fascism . . . Democracy . . .' You know the line of talk. This fellow, I suppose, makes his living by writing books against Hitler. But what did he do before Hitler came along? And what'll he do if Hitler ever disappears? He *means* it. Not faking at all – feels every word he's saying. He's trying to work up hatred in the audience, but that's nothing to the hatred he feels in himself. Every slogan's the gospel truth to him. If you cut him open all you'd find inside would be Democracy–Fascism–Democracy. Interesting to know a chap like that in private life. I'd stopped listening to the actual words of the lecture. But there are more ways than one of listening. I shut my eyes for a moment. The effect of that was curious. I seemed to see the fellow much better when I could only hear his voice. Hate, hate, hate. Let's all get together and have a good hate. It gives you the feeling that something has got inside your skull and is hammering down on your brain. But for a moment, with my eyes shut, I managed to turn the tables on him. I got inside *his* skull. It was a peculiar sensation. For about a second I was inside him. At any rate, I felt what he was feeling. I saw the vision he was seeing. And it wasn't at all the kind of vision that can be talked about. What he's *saying* is merely that Hitler's after us and we must get together and have a good hate. But what he's *seeing* is something quite different. It's a picture of himself smashing people's faces in with a spanner. Fascist faces, of course. And it's all OK because the smashed faces belong to Fascists. You could hear that in the tone of his voice.[1]

This lecturer is sincere. He does disparage the enemy. Yet, something is wrong. He is moved by something more than just the nefariousness of Fascism. The indignation is motivated. It serves to reconcile two clashing needs: for moral respectability and for aggression, the latter being a need openly indulged by Fascism. Verbal assault underwritten by moral superiority (and the posture of potential victim) is the closest he can come. It is obvious enough that the militant virtue of one whose liberal politics mask a Fascist psychology is not what it seems. A strong intuitition says the same for his indignation. The Fascist was a uniquely deserving fall-guy in this covert drama. There is no lack of successors.

– REAL EMOTION –

In what they do and how they think, people are not always true to what they feel. Yet neither does the heart always feel truly. Emotion can mislead people because it is itself susceptible to a variety of errors. In the most straightforward case, an emotion (such as Othello's jealousy) may be ill-founded in that it is occasioned by false suppositions about the thing at which it is directed. But there are other possibilities. Emotions are not always quite what they seem, especially to those in their thrall. Misidenti-fication of an emotion, confusion with another, can occur when the true cause and reason for it is unclear (as when lust is taken for love). On the other hand, one may be clear about the reason for an emotion but still unclear about its cause: what makes a man react with anger to a minor slight or obstruction at home (and with such anger) may be his antagonism at greater slights and frustrations he has had to swallow elsewhere. Or, what the emotion is about (and the reason for it) may differ from what causes it, and differ in kind, not just in locus: a state of exhaustion may make demanding tasks seem more formidable than they normally would to the point that the prospect of them induces fear; conversely, drunken-ness can induce hubristic confidence and zest.

These are some ways a person can be wrong about his emotions, about what emotion it is or about its objects, reasons or causes. They are problems of recognition (Why am I angry? Why am I angry at that? Is my interest friendly concern or envious probing?). However, there is another way that emotions can play us false. Some emotions can be factitious, not just elusive as to their identity or deviant as to their true causes, reasons or objects. A factitious emotion fails to be a real example of the sort of emotion it seems to be, as opposed to an example that is real enough but just misleading as to its identity or in one of the other ways mentioned. Thus, in the affection of a friend who becomes a friend indeed when he is a friend in need, something is amiss. Even if this fresh fondness is unfeigned, its origin is suspect. And it seems compromised by this. Again, fake anger isn't necessarily faked anger and is the more alarming for that. There are colloquial ways of registering this worry about certain ostensible cases of emotion (be they occurrent or dispositional): people are said to 'work themselves into' or 'conjure up' a state of a given emotion, or to cherish or nourish a given sentiment and perhaps to 'savour' or even 'wallow' in it; we can distinguish 'forced' (also 'shrill') sentiment, 'guilt trips', unctuousness, sententiousness, over-earnestness and the like. And where this is suspected, authenticity is doubted. One is presented here more with the image of the emotion, with virtual emotion. Sentimentality is a prominent special case of this. It turns emotions into caricatures of themselves and robs them of their seriousness. Here, due consideration is denied the object and it is portrayed strictly so as to arouse and nurse the sweeter or more darkly alluring kinds of feeling. Yet such purposeful, sanitising portrayal subverts the emotions themselves, for to recognise devotion or respect or love as sentimental is to decline to acknowledge it as real devotion or respect or love. Emotion is not schmaltz (and conversely).

Many emotions, then, can take both degenerate and non-degenerate forms. They can be more apparent than real. The question is what exactly is amiss in such cases. Before attempting an answer, however, the pre-reflective intuitions need some filling in and sharpening.

– SYNTHETIC EMOTION: A MODEL CASE –

Suppose there are two people of contrary character. There is Nick, who is ill at ease with others and over-anxious to please. He can't abide silence and has to maintain a barrage of constant, random banter. Rick, on the other hand, is ruminative, laconic and doesn't suffer fools gladly. When their professional circumstances force them together Nick finds Rick perversely unforthcoming and even hostile – thankless company and, frankly, intimidating. For his part, Rick finds Nick an irritating twit. Not surprisingly, they bring out the worst in each other: insistent nervous chatter confronts bristling silence. Their working relationship suffers. However, their company has a resourceful Human Resources Officer. Without their knowledge the officer medicates both men with a new psychotropic drug called Amity. Their perceptions of one another remain, but their mutual responses are wonderfully transformed. Thus, despite Nick's admittedly pathetic foibles, Rick warms to him. Irritation and disdain yield to bemused indulgence. On the other hand, Rick's ominous silences no longer prevent Nick from dubbing him somehow likeable. As if by grace, an unaccountable fondness arises on both sides, and the working relationship prospers.

Is this new-found cordiality a case of real fondness (and derivatively, is their relation one of genuine friendship?). Fondness does sometimes flourish or arise in inauspicious circumstances, where surprising though it may be, fondness it is. There need be no doubt of that or any reason not to welcome it – on the contrary. Yet the effect, at any rate, of Amity seems no different from these anomalous warmings-to and friendships. The difference seems to lie not in the sentiment, what and how the people feel towards another, but in the origin of the sentiment, which in this case is unknown to those affected by it. And even this difference may not seem so great. For the possibility of fondness against the grain of the relevant appraisals shows that this emotion, unlike some others (for example, guilt, pride, disappointment), is minimally constrained by the host's actual appraisals. The causes needn't double as reasons in these grace-like instances. But then why should the grossly causal role of Amity make any difference?

– DIAGNOSIS –

It would seem that the status of some instances of emotion – their status as genuine occurrences of the emotions they seem to be – depends on their source. In other words, a state can resemble the occurrent state of a given emotion and yet not be a genuine form of it or of any emotion. Not all emotion-like states or occurrences are proper instances of emotions. How can a state or occurrence be emotion-like and yet fall short? What is misidentified in this case is not the kind of emotion or its object but emotion as such. The notion of an imitation or dummy case of an emotion is also normative: such an emotion is inferior, not to be taken seriously in quite the way real emotions of the given kind are to be taken seriously. It is more an unwitting inner rhetoric.

So, what is the underlying lack? Normally an emotion of a given type involves a characteristic valuation of what it is about, a valuation that presents itself both as a good reason for the emotion and (therefore) as its cause. Now, the valuations evinced in non-genuine occurrences of an emotion are in some sense not really made. In other words, the lack lies in the failure of the putative emotion to be the particular concern with its object that it purports to be, that is, that an emotion of the kind in question is. The true source of an emotive state of this sort must, then, lie elsewhere than in the appropriate valuation of its object.

This is what makes such emotions treacherous guides to the behavioural dispositions of the person professing them (for example, resolution that melts at the first touch of temptation, love that fails of devotion, and so on). If an emotion is avowed and a given valuation is appropriate to it then the failure to embrace this valuation – really to have the called-for attitude – puts the emotion, and the person, at fault. People can feel this fault in themselves, that is, that they have only seemed to rise to the occasion emotionally ('Was I really so sorry?', 'Am I actually interested in this?', 'Am I as committed as I thought?'). I can realise the appropriateness of the valuation, acknowledge it as true – 'That deserves my care' – and I may presume this amounts to my accepting it. But I can be wrong in presuming this. How one could hold a valuation to be appropriate and yet not make it is an instructive question which I will eventually try to answer.

– THE SCOPE OF THE DIAGNOSIS –

How plausible is this preliminary diagnosis? For a start, it is important to emphasise that the fault I am alleging in counterfeit emotions is not that of ordinary insincerity or dissembling. The host to the token emotion sincerely believes he is sincere. He is not just giving the appearance of having the emotion; he himself is subject to the appearance of it. He, so to speak, believes in the emotion, regards it as the real article. Where this happens a person is deluded about what his relations are to the relevant parts of the world and about what kind of person he is. The problem is how something which at the time feels for all the world like E could fail to be E? Often, indeed, it can't. Drugs can induce fear that really is fear regardless of how it is produced or of the appropriateness of its objects. A colour is no less feared for being feared phobically. And the same for lust or euphoria: lust engendered by an aphrodisiac might be indiscriminate but there needn't be anything unconcupiscent about it. And a pathetic fleeting moment of euphoria in a miserable person can still be euphoric, needn't be bitter-sweet, which is why repetitions may be sought by any means (for example, drugs).

But is it the same with, say, affection? The contrast emerges if we imagine Nick and Rick discovering the source of the change in their responses. In one respect this would make no difference. Under Amity, Nick and Rick do experience at least feelings of affection. Although the discovery that the feelings are due solely to doses of Amity needn't, perhaps couldn't, remove the feelings induced by the drug, it would clearly make a difference. It could alter what these feelings amounted to for them. The affectionate feelings could no longer be regarded as fondness or affection, the proper bond of friendship. 'He is dear to me' could not be true of one who knew that this sentiment could be created or destroyed by the popping or not popping of a pill. (This is one reason for denying that emotions consist in feelings of them.)

Perhaps it will be objected that someone could truly say 'Whenever I am on the drug I like him' without just meaning 'I feel (it feels as if) I like him then.' In other words, drugging can create genuine liking. To test the plausibility of this, let us push this indifference to cause to its limit and suppose that Rick and Nick not only realise that their sentiments are pharmacological artefacts but actually take to medicating themselves with the drug. In one way, there is even an improvement, since now at least the feelings owe to the choices of the agents themselves. (Marriage-counselling could be relegated to the rubbish-heap of history.) But the trouble is this: either their motive for self-dosing is that they like one another or it is utilitarian. Ex hypothesi it is not the former, for if it were the drug would obviously be redundant. But if administered with a utilitarian reason (such as the company's reason for surreptitiously dosing them) each party gives the other a strictly instrumental status. But that valuation of a person is inconsistent with the valuation that makes for affection and indeed is inimical to it. The ascription of fondness seems incorrect and even ironic when so motivated, notwithstanding their sus-ceptibility to feelings of fondness. Feelings of affection have been induced with an ulterior purpose (for example, to work efficiently together) and a purpose not of the kind that it belongs to affection to inspire in people. This shows that having affection does not consist just in having feelings of affection. Indeed, the manipulation of feelings, especially affectionate feelings, for purposes alien to them is incompatible with what real fond-ness would permit towards a person. The induced feelings constitute a parody, even a debauchery, of affection proper.

(Why some sorts of emotion allow for factitiousness whilst others do not is a question I will leave hanging.)

– THE CORE: A CONFUSION OF COGNITIONS –

To be carried any further, these preliminary reflections must be viewed in a broader context. The lack I have been diagnosing starts, I suggest, with an anomaly in the cognitive structure of the putative emotion-occurrence. At its most general, a cognitivist conception of emotion holds that emotions embody (or result from) some sort of representation of what the emotion is about. A potentially emotive picture of this may, as we know, be judgemental or pre-judgemental. It may be a view reached and actively endorsed, a belief, behind which we put our weight, so to speak. Or it may be an apprehension that suggests itself, insinuates itself on the mind unasserted (as in fantasy). Seeming is not believing. Even if such construals fail to explain the possibility of irrationality in emotions (see Chapter 2), they *are* a key to their authenticity or integrity – or lack of it. It is actually here that construal comes into its own as an explanatory resource.

What is important about this sort of Gestaltist representation – likening-to, portraying-as – is that it falls short of believing *while still resembling it*. Entertaining a view of something is not *taking* that view of it, although presenting a thing in a certain light does make it *seem* that way. A construal does not actually require me even to consider whether things are as I am presenting them to myself, let alone to satisfy myself that they are. However, if I am unaware that what I am doing is construing rather than considering or affirming, I am not in a position to distinguish my construal from a belief. My appreciation of how fearsome the Boss appears is not then distinct for me from an appreciation that the Boss is to be feared. But this makes it easy, if not inevitable, to treat the construal *as* a belief. That is, I haven't let myself enquire what the Boss is really like, so my impulsive and perhaps fanciful picture is all I have to respond to. This is a potent illusion: I have a facsimile of a belief that is capable of magnetising feeling and passing as genuine emotion. Real feelings are readily and frequently evoked towards a thing by an image of that thing, for example, a stereotype, a caricature or an idolization. But, as we shall see, real emotion can demand actual belief.

For many emotions, feelings of the emotion engendered by a construal constitute a perfectly unproblematic case of that emotion (as noted above in connection with Nick and Rick).[2] Felt fear is fear. Here, genuineness is indifferent to causation. A drug, not to mention a construal of its object as fearsome, can evoke the real article.

However, this does not seem true of all emotions. In the imagined case of Nick and Rick, genuineness was seen sometimes to depend not just on content (how one felt) but on cause (how one came to feel that way). There, the integrity of some emotions was undermined if they originated in pharmacology rather than in appraisal.[3]

A finer question is whether construal as distinct from affirmed appraisal can ever be similarly inadequate. Do emotions sometimes require outright affirmation as their cognitive source? Consider rejoicing. I can think of a reprieve as my deliverance without thinking that I have been reprieved, as when I wonder whether I will be. However, I cannot rejoice at being reprieved unless I actually accept that I have been. A person cannot sanely rejoice in something they do not suppose to have happened. Of course, I could rejoice in the prospect of a reprieve but, again, only if I believe to be in prospect. Again, I could be lightened by or even wax euphoric about the very idea of reprieve; but my joy here is from what I believe this deliverance would mean to me. Similarly, where I believe something has already been realised, I cannot go on hoping for it; hope then becomes joy. Relief at means relief that. These examples suggest that for some emotions there is a requirement of belief, as distinct from construal.[4]

So far, we have two results: some though not all emotions can occur factitiously (be more apparent than real). And some though not all emotions require a cognitive origin in belief, as distinct from construal. These two facts are related. What is the deceiving likeness between real and apparent emotion in the simplified examples involving Nick and Rick?

In the first place, I suggest, emotions which are capable of artificiality become artificial partly by being sustained by construals rather than by beliefs, where beliefs are what is really required. Suppose an emotion is evoked by construal in the absence of appropriate belief: so transfixed and beguiled am I by the very thought of deliverance, that I start to feel relieved (as if I had been reprieved). At the moment that is as far as my state goes; I think of myself as freed but neither think that I am in fact free or that I am not. Here the construal is entertained not in face of the relevant beliefs but in place of them. Now, this creates the possibility of mistaking what is but a construal for committed belief, for confusing a portrayal with a conviction. Then construal would be the covert cognitive source of the emotion. My emotive state would lack, whilst seeming to have, the backing in judgement required by the given emotion-type and normally expected of it.

In the second place, factitious emotions are states or episodes which really do feel like the emotion in question. Or, they do not feel so unlike the way it typically feels to have that emotion (as depression feels unlike elation or relief but not so unlike disappointment) as to preclude identification with it .[5] They are feelings of the kind someone may have who really does have the emotion. They are that aspect of the emotion but no other – the sound and the fury without the true signification. What in particular they are not is that aspect with its correct provenance. This means they do not proceed just from the beliefs, mainly appraisals, that are requisite to the kind of emotion in question and that are capable of evoking such feelings. One is subject to feelings (for example, guilt) of the sort one is liable to have as a result of holding a certain belief (for example, that one is grievously at fault), except that here the feelings do not originate in this belief and one does not even hold it. But the presence of the feelings can encourage a false impression that the appropriate beliefs are held. Even the behavioural dispositions characteristic of the emotion may manifest themselves, but also as deviantly caused. This is the way the appearance of an instance of an emotion is created without the reality.

– The Motivational Core –

How is that possible? How can sentiment get aroused by something inappropriate to arouse it? In what ways is it that anything other than a proper reason could be its cause? (If I don't think I am at fault, what can induce me to feel guilty?) How, especially, could a reason that is downright incompatible with the belief that tends to evoke the feeling in genuine occurrences of the emotion succeed in evoking it in the counterfeit instances of that emotion?

To clarify this, we must examine the sources of factitious emotion. An ingenuous emotion is concerned specifically with its object and caused specifically by this concern. It results directly from how one appraises the object. If genuinely affronted, what occupies me is the affront, and I am affronted (and perhaps feel affronted) because of that. Now, desires in turn can have a role in this causation as causes of the valuations directed at the object. Sometimes this proximate causal background of desire is particularly clear, as in disappointment, jealousy, relief: in each case something was wanted.

However, this role for desire, in which it is directed on to the emotion's object, is vulnerable to a quiet dislocation. The royal road to factitious emotion, the form of its misbegotten causation, is the need for the emotion and the desire to have it. Why misbegotten? A desire to attain to a sentiment is not a desire that is concerned directly with the ostensible object of that sentiment. (A need to host a sentiment centres on oneself, not on anything else.) Should a desire of this form be what leads one to the sentiment, then one's concern for the object per se is dislodged from its place as cause. To have an emotion because one wants to have it is not to have it because of what it is properly about. There is something one wants the emotion for, a role it is to play; and this may have nothing to do with the desires proper to the given emotion and may even be contrary to them.

Two questions arise at this point. (1) Whence this cuckoo's egg? – Why does false emotion occur at all? That is, what inspires the wish for certain emotions? (2) And, again, how is it possible? How can the desired effect be achieved by the wrong sort of cause?

(1) Desires for specific emotions can have an indefinite range of motives. These cannot be delimited but I will examine some of the more important candidates. There seem to be at least two general kinds of thing people could want from emotion, an experience or a relation. In the first case the wish is to undergo the emotion and savour the feelings that come with it or to satisfy curiosity about them, much in the way that people try out drugs for the sensations or even feelings they induce. The wish to taste triumph is distinguishable from the wish for the undoing of one's foe. (Where the wish to prevail issues from a wish to gloat, foes may be sought or set up who are of no real interest in themselves.) The feelings that many emotions incorporate, especially in their extremities as passions, offer distinctive thrills, transports, glows, palpitations and releases. For there are attractions of mode as well as of content: the fervent, the intense, the gripping, the consuming, the jarring, the delicate, the fleeting, the glowing, the strange, the sweet, the dark. Moreover, affect as such may be at a premium to someone who is bored or phlegmatic. In short, many feelings, because of their subjective qualities, have a power of charm. I will term charm the Narcissistic motive.

The second general sort of motive for wanting an emotion focuses on the fact of having it, that is, on what it is rather than on what it is like. What matters here is that this should be my emotion – in particular that my circumstances or relation to others should be of the kind to evoke or provoke this in me. For, the fact that my emotion is such-and-such creates a stance or role for me in relation to its object or evoking circumstance. This owes to the judgemental aspect of the emotion, namely to the appraisal of its object that is implicit in the emotion. I can only be offended by offensive treatment; so if I'm offended by you, your conduct towards me must have been shabby. (And what does that say about you and your whole attitude to me, and so on?) The character of my emotion can place me at advantage, morally or socially, or it can console me or reassure me about the kind of person I am. Where a particular emotion is wanted out of a concern for one's lodgment in the world or for self-regard, the motive could be termed Dramaturgical.

The structure of Dramaturgical motivation is the more complicated.

Choice will centre on emotions that promise advantage of power (for example, pity), moral advantage (for example, forgiveness, righteous anger) or that reassuringly affirm desirable personal qualities (for example, compassion, remorse). However, one of the reasons for needing to assume a given emotional stance can be the presence of another emotion that rates as unworthy and that is best expressed in disguised form. The trappings of one emotion can serve to mask another: righteous indignation rather than envy or sheer spite; zealous commitment to a cause that offers a feeling of belonging or of transcendence of the commonplace and the compromised; pity instead of disdain; solicitous concern as opposed to prurient fascination. Notice that the masking emotions tend at once to resemble and to deny the masked emotions.

Where this kind of screening occurs there is a temptation to assimilate the masking emotion to the masked one and treat the case as in effect one of dissembling – to view the mask as a masquerade. The indignation is all an act, it will be said, and the emotion is really just plain spite. It may be that the real emotion is spite but this doesn't make spite the only emotional state, the rest being deceit (although that can happen). The truth is more complex. That the indignation isn't genuine doesn't make it mere pretence. I may believe myself to be indignant and in unleashing vituperation I may feel perfectly confident rather than vulnerable and edgy, as I would be if straining to seem convincing. Wronged but in the right, I can abandon myself in feeling and in expression to a robust and triumphal rancour denied to its poor relation, simple spite. Indignation is, and therefore feels, different (and better) than sheer spite, although of course the appropriate framework of belief is required to make that difference. There is a real emotional state, a state of feeling, resembling indignation (in how I identify it and in how it feels); so while it is a facilitating pretext for my spite, it isn't just a pretext.

It might seem that if the righteousness does not reduce to mere spite, then it must indeed be real indignation, that there is no room for an intermediate, counterfeit version. After all, I both view myself as indignant and feel indignant. How can this fail to be the real article?

(2) To answer this, we must turn to the second question introduced above: how can an emotion be evoked by an inappropriate cause? My answer, of course, is that no emotion proper can arise if the cause is wrong. But a facsimile can be, and it consists in feelings of the emotion and also sometimes the (deluded) belief that one is actually having just this emotion. The problem is how this much can be achieved without achieving more, that is, a genuine instance of the emotion. For what

alternative causes are there to the beliefs that appropriately found this emotion?

Sometimes mechanical interventions are possible, such as psychotropic drugs or associative conditioning (does Winston Smith really love Big Brother by the closing scene of *1984*?). However there are at least two other devices that are more subtle, applicable to a wider field of emotions, and certainly more common.

The first is by mimicry. By acting the part of one affected by a given emotion, one can actually awaken some of the feeling characteristic of it. The sounds, speech, gestures, demeanour and actions expressive of a state of feeling in another allow us to imagine it. Dancing and acting trade on that. By miming these expressions oneself as comprehensively and truly as possible one can discover the feeling, not just imagine (let alone infer) it. An actor, on or off the stage, can lose himself in a part and where crying is called for find himself crying rather than imitating crying; and actual crying is inseparable from at least a spasm of sorrow, however much one may know there is nothing to sorrow over. The feeling, at least, and its natural bodily expression in particular seem inextricable, as anyone will realise who tries to meet Wittgenstein's challenge to 'Just try to think over something very sad with an expression of radiant joy.'[6] Perhaps the explanation is this: 'what we feel in an emotion state is the expressive set of our body'.[7]

Without realising it a person can be carried along in the enactments of an emotion by social pressure and example or by the hidden hand of personal need to the point of becoming accessible to feelings of that emotion. Nothing is then easier than to mistake these promptings for the emotion, beliefs and all, which one has a motive for wanting, and for presuming the emotion to be the cause of the expressive behaviour that in fact primed the feelings.

This can be assisted by the belief the person forms as to what his or her emotion is. Feelings, and not only those of bodily states, are sometimes indeterminate across a given range of emotions. They may be vague or mixed. A feeling of inchoate hostility ('You do things to me!') may be indefinite as between fear, hate, or envy. One and the same person may evoke a bewildering jumble of admiration, gratitude, resentment and fear. The wish that one's emotion should be such and such can foreclose on this indeterminateness in the shape of a wishful belief about what it all means. What is felt henceforth will be affected by this consolidated view of what is felt. For a person's belief about the identity of his or her emotion has self-confirming resources. To take my attitude to be love, resentment or remorse is to try to take the attitude of love, resentment or remorse. That is, I will expect the object to have qualities appropriate to my presumed emotion, and expecting them, I will tend to find them. I will tend to be sensitive to anything about the object that is consonant with the emotion and oblivious or resistant to anything else. This, in turn, will tend to encourage the beliefs actually required by the emotion in question. Ostensibly convincing grounds for the emotion will take shape. To the extent that this succeeds, the avowed emotion is at least sincere, however ill-founded.

The wish for an emotion also has an independent capacity to make it seem that this emotion really is the one felt. It motivates a person wherever he can to construe his experience in a way that invites the desired emotion. This is distinct from the aforementioned procedure of selective noticing instigated by belief. Construal, it will be recalled, is a matter not of what is picked out but of what is made of it, how it gets represented. And entertaining a view of something is not affirming that view of it, even though entertaining the view of something as x can make it seem x. As suggested earlier, this sort of Gestaltist representation (likening to, portraying as) falls short of believing whilst still resembling it. So construal does not actually require me even to consider whether things are as I am presenting them to myself, let alone to satisfy myself that they are. But if I am unaware that what I am doing is construing rather than considering and affirming, I am not in a position to distinguish my construal from a belief. My savouring of the prospect of freedom can then seem little different to me from the expectation of it. But that makes it easy, if not inevitable, to treat the construal as a belief. That is, I haven't got around to (or let myself) enquire what is really in prospect, so my impulsive picture is all I have to respond to. This is a potent illusion: I have a facsimile of a belief that is capable of magnetising feeling and passing as genuine emotion.

What we are confronted with is a motivated image of a person, a group or a situation that is confabulated and sustained without any real effort to comprehend or weigh. At the time, such a portrayal will be so beguiling, so urgent, and the difference between belief and construal elusive enough, that the compromised origins of the portrayal will be well-nigh invisible, perhaps for a lifetime. This is the anatomy of, for instance, zealotry, be it blatant or subtle, unfashionable or 'correct'. Because the zealot's cognitive attitude is not one of belief but only of storytelling, and because he or she declines in practice to wonder about the truth of the matter, there is a sense in which his or her attitude towards the target is not serious.

Consider people repeating slogans or citing received ideas they do not understand and for whom curiosity on this point would amount to apostasy. If the claims made by the ideas or slogans were what really mattered, it would be vital to know whether they were sound. That this should be the wrong question to raise suggests that the real source of the concern is not the one which belongs to the emotions evinced. To be sure, real *feelings* are readily and frequently evoked towards a thing by an image of that thing, for example, a stereotype, a caricature or a fantasy. However, real emotion, where it can fail, demands actual belief.

– THE COUNTERFEIT VS THE RENEGADE –

This is not to say that any emotive state that is charged with feeling but lacks a suitable judgemental basis is a factitious emotion. Irrational guilt is not pseudo-guilt. Even if it is a case of unfounded guilt feelings, it is still a suffering from guilt. If I *cannot* be freed of the feelings, the guilt is real enough but irrational; if I won't *let* myself be freed of these groundless feelings, what I am suffering from is not guilt.

Exactly how, then, does internally staged emotion differ from internally irrational emotion (discussed in Chapter 2)? When I am the victim of a subjectively irrational emotion such as phobic fear, my feelings of alarm are in open conflict with what I take myself to believe, namely, that there is nothing to fear. When I am the agent of a cultivated emotion, my feelings harmonise with what I take myself to believe. (When I am just absorbed in a feeling, such as anxiety, gloom or serenity, without apparent reason, there is no belief with which my feeling either harmonises or clashes.) So one difference lies in the respective frameworks of second-order beliefs in which the feelings are set. Bewildering though irrational and non-rational emotions may be, they are actually less confused than staged emotions are: my beliefs are what I think they are, so that at least I know that I don't know what the cause is.

Their causation is the other thing that distinguishes irrational (and non-rational) but *bona fide* emotions from synthetic ones. The latter are motivated, they are summoned or sustained to a purpose; and the desire to have them is crucial to their causal history. By contrast, irrational emotions (and unfocused atmospheres) are spontaneous. They are not designer emotions, and it is not essential to them that they serve the person's interests; indeed, such emotions are as often visitations from the gods as gifts from them. Their causal history is apt to be quite obscure, often psychodynamic or even physiological in nature and certainly not reliant on the wish for them.

It is true that causal innocence is not quite as simple as I have made it sound. The generation of given emotions is central to certain forms of therapy, such as role-playing and psycho-drama, not incidental to them. Suppose that someone enters one of these therapies to 'learn' how to be, or to let himself be, angry, as might happen in assertiveness training or in a programme of building self-esteem. Suppose that by enacting encounters, people can meet their anger as never before. Does the fact that the process is deliberate and this effect desired render the emotion synthetic? Is this just a narcissistic shooting of the emotional rapids, an affect-adventure?

These are not easy questions, and there is no one answer. If a person chooses to enter or create a situation that really is of the sort evocative of the emotion in question, then the cognitive conditions for the emotion are satisfied and if the response is forthcoming it is not factitious. After all, the encounter will be with real people and the role played may be of the sort really played outside the Group. It is not a stage drama. That the setting is rigged need not make it wholly artificial. In fact, the setting need only *resemble* a full, natural encounter of the kind, as is the case in ritual (see Chapter 2).[8] Nor does a person's complicity in another's attempt to coax them into *expressing* an emotion that is antecedently there (or latent) impugn the emotion. In these exercises, the desire for the emotion causes it at one remove; it plays an *indirect* part in the genesis of the emotion. On the other hand, it is there, and there are risks. To the extent that the person just pretends to himself that the circumstances making for the emotion are really at hand, any feelings generated are just sound and fury.

– A Plea in Defence –

Does this have to be bad? Does genuineness of emotion matter? – Why not indulge desirable feelings? To these normative questions about factitious emotion there are several replies:

1. The ostensible emotion misrepresents the agent both as to his true emotion and as to his true values. Even though this usually occurs spontaneously and unreflectively, a (sane) person is not incapable of identifying and resisting it in himself and is letting himself go when he doesn't. So it is akin to deceitfulness.
2. The dangers of self-misrepresentation to oneself and to others who

have to respond to the appearance one gives are many. Reality can become a Sword of Damocles.

3. To sustain the subjective appearance of having a given emotion, which requires having the relevant beliefs, may require misrepresenting the world outside the self. Unflattering distortions are apt to be unfair and cruel, and flattering distortions of one thing are apt to be sustained by contrastingly unflattering distortions of other things. Herein lies the sinister potential of sentimentality, for example. 'The qualities that sentimentality imposes on its objects are qualities of innocence.' These objects arouse sentiment as exemplars of 'sweetness, dearness, littleness, blamelessness and vulnerability'. Often, however, 'the unlikely creature and moral caricature that is someone unambiguously worthy of sym-pathetic response has its natural counterpart in a moral caricature of something unambiguously worthy of hatred.'[9]

4. Because factitious emotions are not motivated by the appropriate appraisals (or dispositions to these), they lack the function that is frequently the warrant for emotion as distinct from dispassionate rational appraisal, namely, creating an immediate urge to act in accord-ance with the appraisal.[10] If this is the role of emotion, factitious emotion is a betrayal of it.

5. What is characteristically desired in a case of factitious emotion is properly grounded feeling (indignation that is justified, the thrill of real triumph, and so on). But that is just what it is not. And feelings grounded primarily in the wish for properly grounded feelings are not what is wanted. Counterfeit emotion necessarily can't get what it wants. Of course these considerations do not show that construing experience in a way conducive to a desired emotion is of itself sufficient to impugn the emotion; nor that it is necessarily a bad thing. For instance, the disposition always to try to view a friend or loved one in a favourable light, to put a generous or at least forgiving construction on what they do, belongs to the loyalty that is integral to such relation-ships. Potentially damning evidence is indeed not to be accepted and weighed impersonally. These construals need not always amount to belief; they more represent one's faith in the person. But they are also chosen: this person knows what he or she is doing. That means that while they nourish affection they also express it. Such construals result from the affection and are not being relied on to engender it. By contrast, construals conducive to an emotion that are treated as a means of eliciting that emotion cannot already be motivated by it and must be motivated in the first instance just by the desire to have this

emotion. But, again, the desire to have it is not itself the concern with its object which makes it that emotion. Nor is the motive for the desire to have it likely to be identical with this attitude to its object (or else this motive would just be that emotion). So the attempt to conjure up emotion by means of construals is necessarily self-subverting and must come down to masking instead.

This conclusion may sound harsh and the argument suspiciously abstract. How and how well does it really work against what look like constructive wishes to have certain emotions? Is the desire to have an emotion necessarily extraneous to the desires proper to that sort of emotion? Love, to take at least one leading example, would seem to include the wish that the beloved be loved by the one who loves. It would also seem to include the wish to wish to love the beloved. (What gives this strange statement its sense is that the idea of unwillingly loving is paradoxical in a way that unwillingly being attracted to or infatuated with are not.)

In 'The Idea of Perfection', Iris Murdoch describes a case of constructive emotional reform:

> A mother, whom I shall call M, feels hostility to her daughter-in-law, whom I shall call D. M finds D quite a good-hearted girl, but while not exactly common yet certainly unpolished and lacking in dignity, pert and familiar, insufficiently ceremonious, brusque, sometimes positively rude, always tiresomely juvenile . . . M feels her son has married beneath him. Let us assume for purposes of the example that the mother, who is a very 'correct' person, behaves beautifully to the girl throughout, not allowing her real opinion to appear in any way. M is an intelligent and well-intentioned person, capable of self-criticism, capable of giving careful and just attention to an object which confronts her. M tells herself: 'I am old fashioned and conventional. I may be snobbish. I am certainly jealous. Let me look again.' Here I assume M observes D or at least reflects deliberately about D, until gradually her vision of D alters. D is discovered to be not vulgar but refreshingly simple, not undignified but spontaneous, not tiresomely juvenile but delightfully youthful, and so on.[11]

Murdoch allows that in practice,

> It might be very hard to decide whether what M was doing was proper or not, and opinions might differ. M might be moved by various motives: a sense of justice, attempted love for D, love for her son, or simply reluctance to think of him as unfortunate or mistaken. Some people might say 'she deludes herself'

while others would say she was moved by love or justice. I am picturing a case where I would find the latter description appropriate.[12]

Let us, too, assume the best about M: she regrets her disdain of D and wishes she could take a more cordial view of her. And this is just because she always wants loving relations with people who enter her personal life (that is, not just because this would please her son or give her peace of mind). Nonetheless, the fact that her reconsideration of D is motivated rather than spontaneous means that she is to some extent coaxing herself. This does put the genuineness of her reappraisals at risk. Is she forcing herself to ignore things that would niggle and prey upon her if she let them? She may come to see how what she had been inclined to find juvenile could with equal justice be found delightfully and refreshingly youthful, but is she actually delighted and refreshed by them? There needn't be any one answer nor always any clear answer to such questions, but they do apply, in principle and in practice.

Depending on what the answers are, there are four distinct things M could be doing. Do any of them allow her to attain actual love for D, love that could be regarded as such by D if she could see into M's mind?

1. In the name of decency, M achieves a revised picture of D, but it doesn't really carry her emotion with it. That is, she comes to see how D deserves what it is not in her heart to give. But this impasse needn't manifest itself if she systematically avoids noticing what she finds distasteful. The eclipse of her aversions by her grasp of how D is likeable removes the obstacle to *believing* she likes her. And she has a motive for believing this. We have already examined how far a person's belief about her emotion can take her. Also, her avoidance of the distasteful things about D, if possible, would require some form of self-deception. Unpromising. Down this avenue she is whistling in the dark.

2. Suppose the answer to the question – how strained and how sincere are her new-found, generous portrayals of D – is: she isn't sure. Since she is well intentioned, she can try to resolve her uncertainty, her fragility of conviction, by extending benefit of doubt. This is the position of good-will, if not yet of faith, which it resembles, since she chooses to assume the constructive view and to pick fault wherever it can be found with the ungenerous view, and she is not unaware of this. This inverse cynicism is the bent-over-backwards position. It

shares a little, but only a little, of the artificiality of (1). And the principle behind it is the same as (3).

3. To avert the problem of contending against actual or possible doubt altogether, M doesn't venture to ask herself what D is really like but at once construes everything about her for the best. There is no benefit of the doubt because the very recognition of doubt is fended off. This is the benign counterpart of the policy of religious or political commitment. It is doubtful whether true loyalty to someone consists in indiscriminately thinking the best of them; but it is uncertain that loving someone is incompatible with founding it on slight of hand. It is not a strategy that could survive recognition. 'I've conned myself into loving you' is obviously self-annulling as a declaration of love. Indeed, it is not clear that self-induced love by *strategy* could survive the inducer's recognition ('I've got myself to love her'). So:

4. The wish to love truly, and not just to seem to, must involve the wish to love on good grounds, if on grounds at all – to love out of causes that are worthy of it. Examples of causes not proper to love or worthy of it would be: for my son's sake (in the case of M); for my conscience's sake (in a heartless but guilty parent); because you remind me of an old flame. (4) at last is the wish that the beloved could accept and therefore which the harbourer of love could afford to acknowledge. Here is the wish – the wish to love truly, that is, for sound causes – that does not detract from the emotion for which it is the wish.

However, can this innocent wish play the part of a motive for love? We noted earlier that to love someone is to want them to be loved by one and for one to want oneself to want this. But the argument that this wish to love is compatible with properly loving was that it just belongs to loving. The condition of its appropriateness is the presence of love. None of this establishes it as a fit antecedent of love. The means required to give this wish effect where love is not already present are set out in (1)–(3), and they seemed rather to prevent it from being a fit antecedent.

Admittedly there is nothing impossible or wrong about wishing to love someone (whether a specified person or not). Can't that wish be given effect? Yes, but only indirectly. The wish to love truly was the wish to love other than on fraudulent, flimsy or disingenuous grounds. This makes truthfulness essential. The only procedure that accords with it is to seek an open view of the person, a view which gives due recognition to all their relevant attributes as well as to all one's responses to these and then to hope for the best. One's heart must be searched, not rigged. One can do much to give the desired emotion a chance, but then it just has to happen, as by grace, or not. And there's no cutting the risk that it won't by attention-management or other self-manipulation. There are some emotions one cannot intend to induce in oneself. Technique cannot replace uncertainty and hope.

– THE INGENUOUS MIND –

Of course the wish to feel comfortable with one's feelings rather than dismayed by them is inevitable. When they threaten not to oblige, is the only alternative an attempt to evoke a preferred sentiment? The motivation for the efforts at emotional reconstruction we have been examining arises from treating ideals extraneous to one's actual emotional responses, and perhaps in conflict with them, as being those one really stands for. It is the unwillingness to acknowledge attachment to values that are affirmed exclusively ('merely') by emotion. The idea that it is unworthy, and just not done, to be envious or ungrateful or jealous or to savour the voluptuous or experience *Schadenfreude* creates the need for acceptable substitutes. Unfortunately, the acceptable substitutes do not lend themselves to this reflexive motivation. Mere facsimiles are all it can deliver.

The alternative to the attitude that makes for counterfeit sentiment, then, would be an attitude which can accept that my values are or include what my emotional responses make them out to be – surprises, warts and all. Here I refuse to refuse to identify with the verdict of my emotions. This reintroduces the spontaneity of sentiment. My emotions must be allowed to take the form they seek to take; and they must be acknowledged as authoritative expressions of part of my actual valuational attitude, as bearing witness to my real beliefs. A certain integrity must be granted even to bad feelings. For, as we have seen, it is futile to try to redirect them.

It seems, then, that a certain passivity or receptivity towards emotion is a necessary virtue. This prospect has always been unwelcome to those who need to exert total control over their lives. Does it really mean abandoning oneself to sentiment, helpless surrender in the arms of one's passions? No. I can acknowledge something as my value without affirming it as the value. I can regretfully prefer push-pin to poetry, that is, treat certain things with greater regard than I think they deserve. The values I recognise needn't be *confined* to those I hold to in my primary emotional responses. Thus, my responses may disappoint, shock, thrill or intrigue me. And that is a form of mental conflict in which I needn't be helpless.

Suppose my response to a friend's generosity is ungrateful (for example, resentful) and that I recognise and regret this. The foregoing discussion does imply that it is not open to me to intervene directly in the offending response. An adroit inner advertising campaign may modify the character of my immediate feelings, but without summoning real emotion. However, something more indirect and difficult is open to me: to try to make myself the kind of person who isn't subject to the offending reaction in the first place. But the motive here is not to clean up my local emotional act; rather, it is to be able to do justice to the friend (or to others generally) by becoming less defensive. Failing this change of character, there remains the resource of self-discipline, that is, of ensuring that at least my actions are better than my heart. In both cases there is an unavoidable risk of failure.

– FALSE EMOTIONS AND INSINCERITY –

In 'Sincerity and Single-Mindedness', Stuart Hampshire identifies as insincere those emotions whose cause is other than what their host supposes.[13] Certainly, false emotions do rely on confusion in their host as to their true sources. The insincerity in this, however, is ambiguous. The charge of insincerity can obscure the important fact that the host's view of his emotion, even when orchestrated by ulterior motives in the ways described, may be perfectly sincere. For the person may be, perhaps must be, oblivious to the true sources and nature of his emotion. *He* is sincere, his emotion is not. The sincerity of his view of himself is part of what makes his emotion insincere, that is, not what it seems. I confidently rejoice that I dote on you, whilst in truth I gloat on your dependence on me.

Hampshire omits to make this distinction because he also thinks that what one's emotion is is a function of what one thinks is its origin: 'If my belief or assumption about the cause of the feeling is displaced by an argument that shows me that the belief or assumption about its cause is unfounded, my sentiment will change also.'[14] This would make reflection on the true causes of one's emotions vital, and is a warning against just accepting them as they come, of trusting them as they present themselves and maintaining no reflective distance from them. Unfortunately, it also seriously overestimates the causal sway over one's emotions of one's belief about their causes (subjective irrationality is a warning against this).

The very contrast between my sincerity of conviction about what my emotion is and why I have it and the potential insincerity of this emotion betrays *limits* to the power that reflection exerts over emotion. We have seen that a person's reflections on his sentiment's sources are only too liable themselves to be guided by the wishes and perspectives generated by other emotions or needs. And self-scrutiny alerted to *this* may leave one only with the division between what one appreciates is the case and what one actually feels. Emotion needn't follow insight.

Suppose it did, however. While the task of self-insight needn't be endless, there is no telling just when it is completed, when collusion or ignorance have been overcome and insight reached. When do I really know what my feelings are responding to? When do I know that I know? But if my grasp of the sources of my emotion is thus constitutionally uncertain, the practice of making my emotions always conditional on such scrutiny would make them forever provisional and me chronically prevaricating. 'I think I hate him'/ 'I probably love you' – the price of sincerity would turn out to be genuineness of emotion! The examined life would not be worth living.

This obliges us to recognise after all the importance of the spontaneity of emotion to its sincerity. The less a sentiment towards something depends on a view of that thing that has been constructed independently of its capacity to evoke this sentiment, the more likely the sentiment is to be genuine. The more antecedent significance an object has – moral, political, social, theoretical or emotional – the more masters there are to please. This means that true emotion demands a capacity for constantly renewable openness to the world and for acceptance of emotion even when it pulls against the diktat of cherished prescription.

Hampshire opposes this ingenuous trust in emotions. He thinks that until I am clear what ideas about the source of my emotion really govern me and what that source is truly like, the emotion risks being insincere or misplaced; and this requires reflection on the sources and on my view of them. Hampshire queries Stendhal's association of this circumspect alertness to the grounds of emotion with northern European cultures in opposition to the enviably spontaneous, un-self-watching southern cultures: ' "Be natural: be like the Spanish and Italians: just feel as you feel" '.[15]

Clearly where an emotion is likely to be in error about its ground such reflection is necessary. But as a ubiquitous and permanent accompaniment of one's emotions, this scrutiny is a mixed blessing. Apart from rendering current sentiment always provisional, it is itself open to self-deceit and so can open the way to counterfeit emotion. Sometimes there is no better or other guide to what one really makes of an object than the emotion it spontaneously arouses. Such considerations underpin the intuition that insistent assessment and reassessment of one's estimate of a thing, the worrying at this common in self-preoccupied people, are not the gates of true emotion. For once, the wisdom lies in the south.

– NOTES –

1. Orwell (1962), pp. 144–8.
2. I offer examples. For extended arguments, see Stocker (1987) and Greenspan (1988).
3. An interesting residual problem that emerges here is why causation matters when it does and why it doesn't when it doesn't.
4. Notice, however, that a knowledge requirement would go too far. I can rejoice at a reprieve I only believe to have been granted (say, a counterfeit fabricated by a sadistic warder to play me up).
5. The case for the independent identifiability of emotion feelings is made by Leighton (1985) and Stocker (1983), and at greater length in Chapters 2 and 7 above.
6. Wittgenstein (1981), p. 508.
7. de Sousa (1980), p. 247.
8. Here is a scene of ritual (an exotic encounter group?) in which there seem no grounds for scepticism about the emotions elicited:

> Kaluli ceremonies are customarily held to celebrate some notable happy event . . . The dances take place at night in the central hall of the longhouse and are performed by the guests for the benefit of their hosts. In the performance, a group of elaborately costumed male dancers take turns dancing and singing in the light of the torches held by the audience. The songs are newly composed and refer to places – streams, hills, gardens, and house sites on the audience's clan lands. These references to their lands remind the listeners of loved ones, now dead or far away, who once lived there. As they listen, the audience falls into a mood of profound nostalgia and pathos. The images of lost loved ones and times past which are evoked by the songs become so poignant that many of the listeners are deeply moved and burst into tears. Then, becoming angry at the anguish they have been made to feel, they leap up, grab a torch from a bystander, and stamp it out on the back of the dancer's bare shoulder. Others leap up supportively from the sidelines, brandishing weapons and yelling war cries, and making terrific clamour. The dancer continues to sing relentlessly amid the pandemonium, without any sign of pain, until his turn comes to an end and he is replaced by another. Dancer follows dancer throughout the night. Each song moves more people to weeping and anger and burning the dancers. The performance finally breaks up at dawn. The dancers then perform an important act: they pay compensation to those in the audience whom they have caused to weep, and everyone returns home in a mood of exuberance.
>
> (Schieffein (1985), p. 113)

9. Jefferson (1983), p. 527. See especially Jefferson's development of the example from E. M. Forster (p. 527ff.).
10. This idea is developed by Greenspan (1988), ch. 6.
11. Murdoch (1970), p. 17.
12. Ibid., p. 18.
13. Ibid., p. 18.

14. Hampshire (1972), p. 247.
15. Ibid., p. 247.

CHAPTER 9

Conclusion:
Emotion, Thought and the Will

While the exclusion or reduction of feeling by cognitive theories is a crippling error, feeling remains a doubtful guide to at least some emotions. Because so many emotions *are* the feelings of them, it is easy to miss those that are not. Because cognitivism is so widely and deeply false, it is hard to appreciate where and how it is true.

This is not the only irony in the relation to thought and feeling in emotions. For the very reason that spontaneity is vital to real emotion, reflection has a proper role in it. The preceding discussion exposes the risk of failing to distinguish belief from the motivated conjurings of imagination in the genesis of one's emotions. This is a practical difficulty as well as a theoretical one. So the need here is twofold: for workaday psychological insight ('Do I really believe this or am I only pretending?') and for a grasp of what emotions are. In serving the latter need, the philosophy of emotion itself has an active, if neglected, part to play in the actual life of the emotions. The preceding discussion, for instance, suggests how emotions which can be just passions (such as fear, dejection, lust or high spirits) can be marshalled and directed by means that the others resist. For imagination (construal), which informs feeling, can be manipulated in a way that belief cannot. Beliefs are not to be summoned at will: I cannot just believe something directly (or try to) as I can just dwell on it, put it out of my mind, or consider it under a certain aspect, more or less vividly (or try to), and thereby alter my feelings. The more tied to reason emotions are, then, the less free we are as to whether we have them. The more they are just feelings, the closer they come to being subject to the will. Real emotions which are tied to beliefs are not available as commodities, to be coaxed, conjured and shaped as desired. To try to obtain them is to lose them. Because they must be spontaneous, they call for the examined life.

Have we restored a place to feeling only to diminish it again? Recall that a person's very wish to achieve the 'right' emotions was animated by a concern with feeling. In the case of the Narcissistic motive this is overt; but even the Dramaturgical motive – the need to cut the right figure – turns on the avoidance of shame, the satisfactions of pride, the solace of affection and the like. And this bears witness to the fact that feelings have value for what they are variously like and confer value on the things that fill us with them. Feeling is what matters most about emotions, their core force. Guilt, for instance, does not assume true gravity unless it mortifies and is felt as a scourge. And nothing is surer to arouse it than an empathic recognition of the violation of feeling inflicted by the offence, an abasement, hurt, desolation or sorrow – the ruin inflicted on tranquillity or delight – and the quality of contempt that deserves. For all the perils and pitfalls of feelings, however, the life unquickened by them would not be worth living. Our understanding of emotion should reflect that.

Select Bibliography

Armon-Jones, C. (1991), *Varieties of Affect*, Harvester Wheatsheaf.

Armstrong, D. M. and Malcolm, N. (eds) (1984), *Consciousness and Causality*, Blackwell.

Beardsley, M. (1978), 'Metaphorical Senses', *Nous*, 12: 3–16.

Bedford, E. (1956), 'Emotions', *Aristotelian Society Proceedings*, LVII: 281–305, reprinted in V. C. Chapell (ed.) (1962), *The Philosophy of Mind*, Prentice-Hall, pp. 110–26.

Ben-Ze'ev, A. (1997), 'Appraisal Theories of Emotion', *Journal of Philosophical Research*, xxii: 129–45.

Blackburn, S. (1984), *'Spreading the Word: Groundings in the Philosophy of Language'*, Oxford University Press.

Bowlby, J. (1973), 'Situations that Arouse Fear', in J. Bowlby, *Attachment and Loss*, vol. II, Viking, pp. 115–60.

Budd, M. (1985), *Music and the Emotions*, Routledge & Kegan Paul.

Cohen, L. J. (1972), 'The Role of Inductive Reasoning in the Interpretation of Metaphor', in D. Davidson and G. Harman (eds), *Semantics of Natural Language*, Dordrecht, pp. 722–41.

Cohen, L. J. (1979), 'The semantics of Metaphor', in A. Ortony (ed.), *Metaphor and Thought*, Cambridge University Press, pp. 64–78.

Conrad, J. (1994), *Nostromo*, Penguin.

Cooper, D. (1986), *Metaphor*, Oxford University Press.

Crimmins, M. (1992), 'Tacitness and Virtual Beliefs', *Mind and Language*, 7: 240–63.

Davidson, D. (1980a), 'Actions, Reasons and Causes', in D. Davidson (ed.), *Essays on Actions and Events*, Oxford University Press, pp. 3–21.

Davidson, D. (1980b), 'Hume's Cognitive Theory of Pride', in D. Davidson (ed.), *Essays in Actions and Events*, Oxford University Press, pp. 277–91.

Davidson, D. (1984), 'What Metaphors Mean', in D. Davidson (ed.), *Inquiries into Truth and Interpretation*, Oxford University Press, pp. 245–65.

de Sousa, R. (1980), 'Self-Deceptive Emotions', in A. Rorty (ed.), *Explaining Emotions*, University of California Press, pp. 283–99.

de Sousa, R. (1987), *The Rationality of Emotion*, MIT Press.

Deigh, J. (1994), 'Cognitivism in the Theory of Emotions', *Ethics*, 104: 824–54.

Dennett, D. (1991), *Consciousness Explained*, Penguin.

Elster, J. (1989), *Nuts and Bolts*, Cambridge University Press.

Fairbairn, W. R. D. (1952), *Psychoanalytic Studies of the Personality*, Routledge.

Farrell, B. (1981), *The Standing of Psychoanalysis*, Oxford University Press.

Flaubert, G. (1971), *Madame Bovary*, Penguin.

Gaus, G. (1990), *Value and Justification*, Cambridge University Press.

Gordon, R. (1987), *The Structure of Emotions: Investigations in Cognitive Philosophy*, Cambridge University Press.

Green, O. H. (1972), 'Emotion and Belief', *American Philosophical Quarterly*, 6: 24–40.

Greenspan, P. (1988), *Emotions and Reasons: An Enquiry into Emotional Justification*, Routledge.

Hampshire, S. (1965), *Freedom and the Individual*, Harper & Row.

Hampshire, S. (1972), 'Sincerity and Single-Mindedness', in S. Hampshire, *Freedom of Mind*, Oxford University Press, pp. 232–56.

Hampshire, S. (1976), 'Feeling and Expression', in J. Glover (ed.), *The Philosophy of Mind*, Oxford University Press, pp. 73–84.

Hume, D. (1955), *A Treatise on Human Nature*, ed. L. Selby-Bigge, Clarendon Press.

Jefferson, M. (1983), 'What is Wrong with Sentimentality', *Mind*, XCII: 519–29.

Kenny, A. (1963), *Action, Emotion and Will*, Routledge & Kegan Paul.

Kramer, P. (1993), *Listening to Prozac*, Viking.

Kraut, R. (1986), 'Feelings in Context', *The Journal of Philosophy*, 83: 642–52.

Lamarque, P. (1994), *Truth, Fiction and Literature*, Cambridge University Press.

Lang, P. (1993), 'The Three-System Approach to Emotion', in N. Birbaumer and A. Ohman (eds), *The Structure of Emotion*, Hogrefe & Huber Publishers, pp. 10–25.

Lawrence, D. H. (1986), *Women in Love*, Penguin.

Lazarus, R. (1982), 'Thoughts on the Relation between Emotion and Cognition', *American Psychologist*, 37: 1019–24.

Lazarus, R. (1984), 'On the Primacy of Cognition', *American Psychologist*, 39: 124–29.

LeDoux, J. (1994), 'Emotion, Memory and the Brain', *Scientific American*, 270: 32–40.

Leighton, S. (1985), 'Feelings and Emotion', *Review of Metaphysics*, 38: 303–21.

Lycan, W. (1988), 'Tacit Belief', in W. Lycan, *Judgement and Justification*, Cambridge University Press, pp. 54–72.

Lyons, W. (1980), *Emotions*, Cambridge University Press.

Madell, G. (1996), 'What Music Teaches about Emotion', *Philosophy*, 71: 63–83.

Mandela, N. (1995), *Long Walk to Freedom*, Abacus.

Marks, I. M. (1969), *Fears and Phobias*, Heinemann.

Miller, G. and Kozak, M. (1993), 'The Three Systems Assessment and the Construct of Emotion', in N. Birbaumer and A. Ohman (eds), *The Structure of Emotion*, Hogrefe & Huber Publishers: 35–53.

Mounce, H. (1978), 'Understanding a Primitive Society', in R. Beehler and A. R. Drengson (eds), *The Philosophy of Society*, Methuen, pp. 59–81.

Murdoch, I. (1970), *The Sovereignty of Good*, Routledge & Kegan Paul.

Nagel, T. (1979), 'What is it like to be a Bat?', in T. Nagel (ed.), *Mortal Questions*, Cambridge University Press, pp. 165–81.

Nash, R. A. (1989), 'Cognitive Theories of Emotion', *Nous* 23: 481–504.

Neill, A. and Ridley, A. (1991), 'Burning Passions', *Analysis*, 51: 106–8.

Neu, J. (1977), *Thought and Therapy*, University of California Press.

Nussbaum, M. (1993), *The Therapy of Desire*, Cambridge University Press.

Oakley, J. (1992), *Morality and the Emotions*, Routledge.

Ohman, A. and Birbaumer, N. (1993), 'Psychophysiological and cognitive-clinical perspectives on emotion', in *The Structure of Emotion*, Hoggrefe & Huber Publishers: 4–9.

Orwell, G. (1962), *Coming up for Air*, Penguin.

Orwell, G. (1978), *Homage to Catalonia*, Penguin.

Pitcher, G. (1965), 'Emotion', *Mind*, 74: 326–64.

Polanyi, M. (1973), *Personal Knowledge*, Routledge & Kegan Paul.

Pugmire, D. (1989), 'Bat or Batman?', *Philosophy*, 64: 207–17.

Pugmire, D. (1994), 'Real Emotion', *Journal of Philosophy and Phenomenological Research*, LIV: 105–23.

Pugmire, D. (1996), 'Conflicting Emotions and the Indivisible Heart', *Philosophy*, 71: 27–41.

Raffman, D. (1993), *Language, Music and Mind*, MIT Press.

Reisenzein, R. (1983), 'The Schacter Theory of Emotion: Two Decades Later', *Psychological Bulletin*, II: 239–64.

Ridley, A. (1995), *Music, Value and the Passions*, Cornell University Press.

Ridley, A. (1997), 'Emotion and Feeling', *Proceedings of the Aristotelian Society, Supplementary Volume* LXXI: 163–77.

Roberts, R. (1988), 'What an Emotion Is: A Sketch', *The Philosophical Review*, 79: 183–209.

Roberts, R. (1996), 'Propositions and Animal Emotion', *Philosophy*, 71: 147–56.

Robinson, J. (1983), 'Emotion, Judgment and Desire', *The Journal of Philosophy*, LXXX: 731–41.

Rorty, R. (1987), 'Unfamiliar noises: Hesse and Davidson on Metaphor', *Proceedings of the Aristotelian Society*, Supplementary Volume LXI: 283–97.

Ross, S. (1984), 'Evaluating the Emotions', *The Journal of Philosophy*, 81: 309–26.

Ryle, G. (1951), 'Feelings', *Philosophical Quarterly*, 1: 193–205.

Sachs, D. (1974), 'On Freud's Doctrine of the Emotions', in R. Wollheim (ed.), *Freud: A Collection of Essays*, Anchor Press, pp. 132–47.

Sartre, J.-P. (1962), *Sketch for a Theory of the Emotions*, Methuen, translated by P. Mairet.

Sashin, J. (1993), 'Duke Ellington: The Creative Process and the Ability to Tolerate Affect', in S. L. Ablon, D. Brown, E. J. Khantzian and J. E. Mack (eds), *Human Feelings*, The Analytic Press, pp. 120–30.

Schieffelin, E. (1985), 'The Cultural Analysis of Depressive Affect: An Example from New Guinea', in A. Kleinman and B. Good (eds), *Culture and Depression*, University of California Press, pp. 101–34.

Searle, J. (1992), *The Rediscovery of the Mind*, University of California Press.

Solomon, R. (1977), *The Passions*, Doubleday (1993 reprint, Hackett).

Stocker, M. (1983), 'Psychic Feelings: Their Importance and Irreducibility', *Australasian Journal of Philosophy*, 61: 5–26.

Stocker, M. (1987), 'Emotional Thoughts', *American Philosophical Quarterly*, 24: 59–69.

Styron, W. (1991), *Darkness Visible*, Jonathan Cape.

Tanner, M. (1976–7), 'Sentimentality', *Proceedings of the Aristotelian Society*, LXXXIV: 127–47.

Taylor, G. (1975), 'Justifying the emotions', *Mind*, LXXXIV: 390–402.

Thalberg, I. (1977), *Perception, Emotion and Action*, Blackwell.

Trigg, R. (1970), *Pain and Emotion*, Oxford University Press.

Wender, P. and Klein, D. (1981), *Mind, Mood and Medicine*, Farrar, Straus & Giroux.

Wilkes, K. (1984), 'Is Consciousness Important?', *British Journal of the Philosophy of Science*, 24: 235–50.

Williams, B. (1973), 'Morality and the Emotions', in B. Williams, *Problems of the Self*, Cambridge University Press, pp. 207–30.

Wilson, J. R. S. (1972), *Emotion and Object*, Cambridge University Press.

Wittgenstein, L. (1953), *Philosophical Investigations*, ed. G. Anscombe and R. Rhees, Blackwell.

Wittgenstein, L. (1967), 'Remarks on Frazer's *Golden Bough*', *Synthese*, 17: 233–63.

Wittgenstein, L. (1981), *Zettel*, ed. G. Anscombe and G. von Wright, Blackwell.

Wollheim, R. (1992), *The Thread of Life*, Cambridge University Press.

Zajonc, R. (1980), 'Feeling and Thinking: Preferences Need no Inferences', *American Psychologist*, 35: 151–75.

Zajonc, R. (1984), 'On the Primacy of Affect', *American Psychologist*, 39: 117–23.

Index